9/99

SPENCER CHRISTIAN'S

World of Wonders

Shake, Rattle, and Roll

THE WORLD'S MOST AMAZING VOLCANOES, EARTHQUAKES, AND OTHER FORCES

Spencer Christian
and Antonia Felix

JOHN WILEY & SONS, INC.

New York • Chichester • Weinheim • Brisbane • Singapore • Toronto

Copyright © 1997 by Spencer Christian and Antonia Felix.
Published by John Wiley & Sons, Inc.
Design by Pronto Design & Production Inc.
Illustrations: Abe Blashko for the illustrations of Spencer Christian and the illustrations on pages vi, 36, 69, 71, 75, 81, 94, 104, and 109 and Jessica Wolk-Stanley for the other illustrations.

The publisher and the author have made every reasonable effort to insure that the experiments and activities in the book are safe when conducted as instructed but assume no responsibility for any damage caused or sustained while performing the experiments or activities in the book. Parents, guardians, and/or teachers should supervise young readers who undertake the experiments and activities in this book.

Library of Congress Cataloging-in-Publication Data
Christian, Spencer.
    Shake, rattle, and roll: the world's most amazing volcanoes, earthquakes, and other forces / Spencer Christian and Antonia Felix.
       p.   cm — (Spencer Christian's world of wonders series)
    Includes index.
    Summary: Examines the powerful forces found in the Earth, with an emphasis on earthquakes and volcanoes.
    ISBN 0-471-15291-9 (paper : alk. paper)
    1. Earthquakes—Juvenile literature. 2. Volcanoes—Juvenile literature.
[1. Earthquakes. 2. Volcanoes.] I. Felix, Antonia. II. Title. III. Series: Christian, Spencer. Spencer Christian's world of wonders.
    QE521.3.C47 1997
    551.2–dc21   97-5541

Printed in the United States of America
10 9 8 7 6 5 4 3 2 1

Contents

Introduction
MEET EARTH, AN OASIS IN THE UNIVERSE

Where do you live? I don't mean just your street and your town and your state, but where in the big—so big it's almost impossible to imagine—space called the universe? For starters, your complete address includes this planet, Earth. Just as your home is part of a neighborhood, Earth belongs to a community of planets that spin around a star, the Sun. This community, called a **solar system,** is just a tiny corner of a huge collection of stars, gas, and dust called the Milky Way **galaxy**. And the Milky Way, your home galaxy, is just one of 50 billion galaxies spread throughout the universe. Every galaxy, including the Milky Way, is stuffed with about 100 billion stars, and countless planets and other bits of matter.

So that's the best description of where you live, but you don't need to include "Earth" or "Milky Way" on your written address. Maybe someday, if people make homes on our Moon or on Mars, you'll have to give your zip code *and* your planet!

Earth is actually just one of nine planets in the solar system. In order, moving outward from the Sun, the planets are Mercury, Venus, Earth, Mars, Jupiter, Saturn, Uranus, Neptune, and Pluto. Unlike the other planets, Earth is home to living things, from ants to trees to strange creatures such as weather forecasters. In a solar system where all the other planets are either too hot or too cold to support life, Earth stands out as an oasis.

In this book, we'll go back billions of years to see how Earth was formed out of the same dust that makes up the stars and everything else in the universe. We'll take a journey inside Earth, to explore what lies beneath the surface, all the way to the core. We'll see how the surface of the planet has changed over millions of years, and how mountains are formed. We'll explore the awesome power of earthquakes and volcanoes and discover hidden events erupting beneath the oceans. Earth may look like a calm, blue oasis from space. But it's actually a restless planet, always changing.

Spencer Christian
123 Weather St.
Anytown, NY 00000
U.S.A.
North America
Earth
Solar System
Milky Way
Universe

USA

32

1

To the Core

JOURNEY TO THE CENTER OF THE EARTH

Imagine you're at the beach, and you want to form a ball out
of sand (you're a little bored). You dig down and get a small
handful of damp, sticky sand and press it into a ball. Then
you gather more and press it around the ball, making it
bigger and **bigger** until
it's the size of a softball. (Then you
throw it at your brother's sand
castle—and you're not bored
anymore!)

Earth was formed gradu-
ally, over more than 100
million years, by a similar
process. Scientists think
that Earth was formed by
accretion, a step-by-step build-up

of matter. All matter pulls together through a force called **gravity**. The building blocks that pulled together to form the planet Earth were the bits of matter in cosmic dust, which stuck together like the grains in your sand ball. These bits included elements such as iron and oxygen. **Elements** are clusters of atoms that cannot be broken down into different kinds of atoms. Also present were **compounds**, which include two or more different kinds of atoms. For instance, water is a compound formed by two elements—hydrogen and oxygen.

These pieces of dust lumped together to form small particles. Particles stuck to each other to form gravel, then gravel became small balls. The small balls grew into larger objects called **planetesimals**. Planetesimals collided with each other, stuck together, and grew and grew until they formed an object the size of Earth today. The planet reached its full size about 4.5 billion years ago.

When the planetesimals collided with the ever-growing Earth, the collisions caused heat inside the planet. A collision puts pressure on an object, and pressure creates heat. Another action that caused Earth to heat up was the breaking apart of certain *atoms* (the smallest units of matter). As they fell apart, they released energy, a process that gives off heat. This process of atoms breaking down is called **radioactivity**, and it still goes on today within Earth.

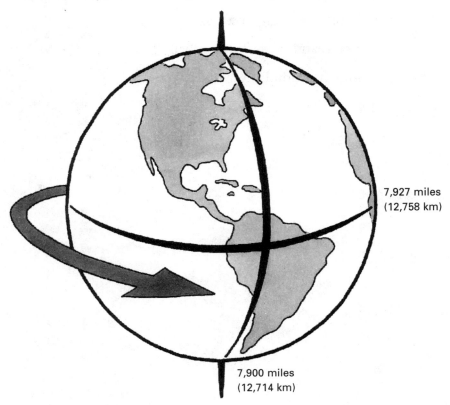

7,927 miles
(12,758 km)

7,900 miles
(12,714 km)

The *Almost* Perfect Globe

arth spins around its *axis*, the imaginary line that runs through the planet from the North to the South Pole, once every 24 hours. The spin of the planet makes it bulge out just a little around the equator and flatten out a bit at the poles. This makes Earth's shape very, very slightly different than a perfect sphere. You wouldn't notice the bulge if you were looking at Earth from space, but the difference is important to pilots, sailors, and surveyors who measure the surface of Earth, and everyone else who needs to know the exact lay of the land or sea. Earth moves in a circular path around the Sun, making one trip every $365\frac{1}{4}$ days. To count in the extra quarter of a day, we add a day to February every fourth year. That year is called a *leap year*.

Crust to Core:
The Structure of Earth

For thousands of years, scientists could only guess what Earth was like inside. But in 1880, the English engineer John Milne created an invention that was to unlock Earth's hidden structure. This invention, the **seismograph**, senses vibrations in Earth caused by earthquakes. It reveals facts about Earth's interior because the speed of an earthquake vibration, called a **seismic wave**, changes when it goes

The seismograph detects and records the vibrations of an earthquake.

How Low Can You Go?

The seismograph is the only way to learn about what lies deep inside Earth because there are no machines that can dig deep enough. The deepest mine in the world goes less than 2.5 miles (4 km) beneath the surface, and the longest drill has only reached 9 miles (15 km) down. But the total distance from the surface to the center of Earth is 3,958 miles (6,370 km)!

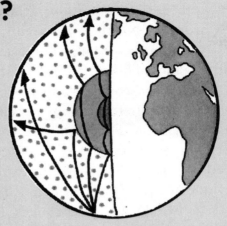

It's all in the vibes: Seismic waves bend or bounce when they pass through different materials within Earth.

through different types of material. By carefully studying the speed and movement of seismic waves, scientists have learned a lot about the structure of Earth. We'll take a closer look at seismic waves in chapter 4.

Crust

The outside layer of Earth is a thin layer of rock called the **crust**. Covering the planet like skin covers the body, the crust is barely 4 miles (6 km) thick in some places. There are two types of crust: continental and oceanic. *Continental crust* ranges from 16 to 56 miles (25 to 90 km) in thickness and in some places is up to 3.8 billion years old. Most continental crust is made up of a granite-type rock that was formed through volcanic action. This rock is lighter than the rock that makes up oceanic crust, so it does not sink into deeper layers of Earth. (We will see how oceanic crust sinks into Earth in the next chapter.) At the heart of the big continents of the world lies the oldest rock on Earth. *Oceanic crust* is thinner than continental crust—less than 4 miles (6 km) thick in some places—and is made of younger rock. All oceanic crust is less than 200 million years old because it is constantly being recycled. This rocky recycling program is also explored in chapter 2.

Minerals and Rock

The building blocks of Earth's crust are 92 elements that normally occur in the form of minerals. A **mineral** is an inorganic (lifeless) substance that contains a definite chemical structure. *Rock* is made out of a mixture of minerals. The most common minerals found in crust are called **silicates**, which are made out of oxygen and the element silicon. Almost 75 percent of Earth's crust is made out of silicates such as feldspar, quartz, mica, olivine, pyroxene, and amphiboles. Silicates are called **rock-forming minerals**. The only other type of rock-forming minerals are **carbonates**, which form rocks called limestone and dolomite.

There are three main types of rocks, which are explored in more detail as we look at mountains, volcanoes, and other structures in upcoming chapters. **Igneous rocks** are formed when magma (melted rock) cools and hardens. Granite, basalt, and obsidian are all igneous rocks. A second type of rock, **sedimentary rock**, is made of particles of sand and mud that have been pressed into layers on lake or sea beds. Sedimentary rocks include sandstone, shale, and limestone. Coal is an organic sedimentary rock that is formed from the remains of plants. The third type of rock is called **metamorphic rock**. These rocks are created when natural forces such as heat, pressure, and the chemicals in gases change the structure of rocks.

Hot Stuff!

Beneath the crust lies a layer of extremely hot rock called the **mantle**. Pressure makes this layer of rock so hot that it flows like a thick liquid. The weight of all the rock above the mantle puts more and more pressure on the rock beneath. That makes the pressure in the deepest part of the mantle very high. The greater the pressure, the higher the heat. The temperature may range from about 950° to 7,500° Fahrenheit (500° to 4,150° Celsius). The mantle is 1,800 miles (3,000 km) thick and is made up of rock that contains a lot of the elements iron and magnesium. The top part of the mantle is solid. As this part moves, it carries along the crust that lies above it. The upper part of the mantle and the entire crust make up the **lithosphere,** which is about 40 to 90 miles (74 to 167 km) thick.

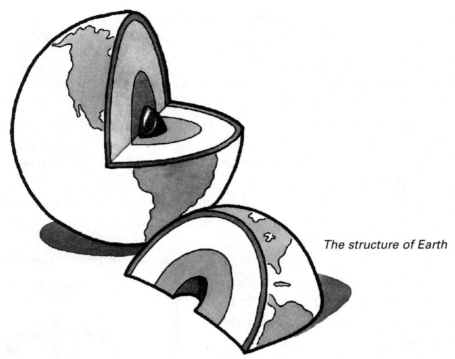

The structure of Earth

Below the mantle lies Earth's **core**. Made up mostly of iron and nickel, the core is solid in the center and liquid on the outside. The liquid outer core is about 1,300 miles (2,100 km) thick, and the inner core, a solid ball, measures about 800 miles (1,300 km) across. The superhot inner core, at nearly 7,000° Fahrenheit (4,000° Celsius), is solid because the pressure is too great for iron and nickel to melt.

Earth as Giant Magnet

The liquid portion of Earth's core acts like a **magnet**. A magnet is an object that attracts materials such as iron and steel toward it. Every magnet has a north pole and a south pole where the power of attraction is strongest. The movement of the hot liquid core of Earth creates a **magnetic** force that surrounds the entire planet. This invisible magnetic field is Earth's **magnetosphere**, which stretches more than 37,000 miles (60,000 km) into space.

Earth's magnetic poles are located slightly off to the side of the geographic North and South Poles (the points around which Earth rotates). Several times in the past 3.5 million years, the magnetic poles have reversed for reasons that scientists do not understand.

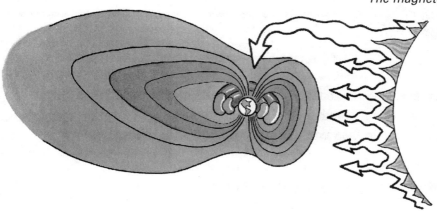

Sometimes the magnetic pole near the geographic North Pole attracts the north pole of a magnet, and sometimes it attracts the south pole. Right now, it attracts the north pole.

You can see the rippling lines of the magnetosphere if you are lucky enough to witness the **aurora borealis**, or northern lights. These beautiful colors are created when particles of energy streaming from the Sun (the **solar wind**) hit either of Earth's magnetic poles. An aurora also occurs at the South Pole. The solar wind also creates the odd shape of Earth's magnetic field. Instead of surrounding the planet in a round shape, the magnetosphere is blown into a tail shape by the solar wind.

Why Does a Compass Line Up with the North Pole?

The moving needle in a compass is a tiny magnet. The north pole of the compass magnet is attracted to the south pole of Earth's magnet, which is near the North Pole. That is why all compass needles point north. Compasses were invented to help sailors find their way around the oceans, but no one understood *why* the needle pointed north until the year 1600. That's when William Gilbert, the physician to Queen Elizabeth I of England, discovered the magnetic poles of Earth in an experiment. Gilbert used a magnet in the shape of a globe to represent Earth. When a compass was placed near the globe, the north pole of the compass needle was attracted to the magnetic south pole of Earth, which was then near the geographic North Pole. From this experiment, he described Earth itself as a giant magnetic globe.

EXPERIMENT

MAGNET-IFY!

Every magnet, from the tiny ones you use to tack notes to the refrigerator to the planet Earth itself, is surrounded by a magnetic field. In this simple experiment, you can see a magnetic field with the help of a few iron filings.

What You Need:
- Two pieces of $8\frac{1}{2}$" x 11" paper, or one piece of construction paper

- Plastic poker chip

- Small plastic or glass bowl

- Iron filings: about 1 tablespoon (available in a hardware store or hobby shop)

- One small bar magnet

What to Do:

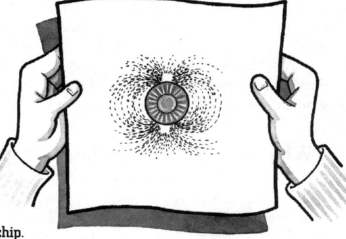

1. Place the poker chip in the center of the paper.
2. Pour the iron filings into the bowl.
3. Carefully tap the bottom of the bowl to sprinkle a thin, even layer of filings onto the paper around the chip. It's okay if filings get on top of the chip.
4. Carefully pick up the piece of paper and slowly lower it over the magnet, so that the chip is positioned directly over the magnet.
5. Gently tap the paper a couple of times to help the filings move.

What Happens and Why:
Iron is a magnetic material. Each tiny piece of iron is attracted to the magnet and moves to line up with its magnetic field. Imagine that the poker chip is Earth. The filings create a visual image of the invisible magnetic field around Earth.

Young Earth: A Hot Spot in Space

For its first few million years, Earth's surface was a churning, hot ocean of **molten** (melted) **rock**. During the planet's molten stage, gases boiled out of the melted mixture and floated above the surface. Melted rock from inside Earth erupted to the surface and blew out steam, water vapor, and gases. The eruption of molten rock from inside Earth is called **volcanic action**. The gases thrown out included carbon dioxide, carbon monoxide, and nitrogen, and they made up Earth's first atmosphere.

When the water vapor rose into the atmosphere, it cooled and changed into liquid water in a process called **condensation**. The water fell to Earth as rain, but for

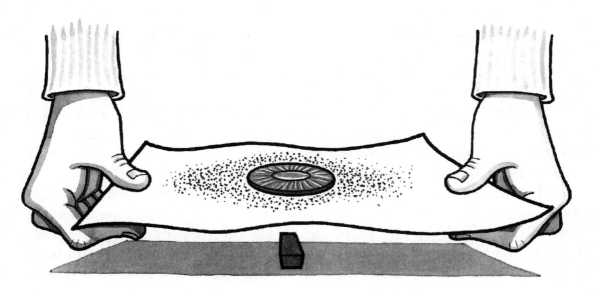

millions of years the surface was too hot for the rain to settle. When it hit Earth, it was instantly heated up into steam and sputtered back into the air. Gradually the surface of the planet cooled, and rain stayed on the ground. As the volcanic action continued to blast water vapor into the air, the rains kept falling and formed rivers and seas.

Oxygen, the gas that human beings need to breathe, did not show up in the atmosphere for hundreds of millions of years. Oxygen was created by the world's first life forms, organisms made out of just one cell each, called *bacteria* or *algae*.

Iron filings patterned over the magnetic field

What Happened to the Dinosaurs?

Scientists still do not know what caused the dinosaurs to disappear from Earth, but they have some ideas. One theory is that many powerful volcanoes erupted, filling the sky with ash and blocking out the sun. Without sunlight, plants could not have grown, and Earth would have become cold. The dinosaurs would not have had any plants to eat, and the temperature would have been too cold to survive. Another theory is that a giant meteor hit Earth, kicking up huge amounts of dust that blocked the sunlight for a long time. Whether it was volcanic activity, a meteor, or some other natural disaster, the dinosaurs no longer roamed the planet after calling it home for nearly 160 million years.

Time Rolls on:
Earth from Age to Age

The history of Earth is divided into four large periods: the Pre-Cambrian Era, the Paleozoic Era, the Mesozoic Era, and the Cenozoic Era.

The Pre-Cambrian Era covers the time from Earth's beginning, about 4.5 billion years ago, up to 570 million years ago. This is the longest era in Earth history—taking up about 90 percent of Earth's timeline.

During the Pre-Cambrian Era the first rock appeared about 3.8 billion years ago, forming the first continents. Algae, the earliest life form, also appeared about 3.8 billion years ago. The oldest **fossils** (imprints of objects in rock) in the world are images of blue-green algae dating from 3.5 billion years ago. These fossils were discovered in Australia and South Africa. Rainwater gathered over the surface during the Pre-Cambrian Era, creating the first oceans.

The Paleozoic Era spans the period from 395 million to 570 million years ago and is divided into six periods. During the oldest period, called the Cambrian period, life-forms developed in the oceans. These creatures included the first vertebrates (animals with backbones), crustaceans (fishes with hard, armor-like bodies), and trilobites (animals with segmented bodies). Trilobites were the most common creature of the sea, and fossils of them are found all over the world. The Cambrian period began 570 million years ago and ended 500 million years ago.

After the Cambrian period came the Ordovician period, which existed from 500 million years ago up to 435 million years ago. In this period, organisms called corals, sponges, and mollusks grew in the oceans. The Silurian period, extending from 435 million years ago to 395 million years ago, brought the first land plants to Earth. In the Devonian period, fishes grew larger and appeared in a variety of shapes. Some fishes developed lungs and became amphibians (animals that can live in the water and on the land). This period lasted 50 million years and ended 345 million years ago.

Next came the Carboniferous period, and the first reptiles crawled around on the lush, swampy Earth. The Carboniferous period lasted from 345 million years ago to 280 million years ago. The final period in the Paleozoic Era was the Permian, in which new types of land plants and many insects developed. This period lasted 55 million years and ended 225 million years ago.

The next era in Earth's history, the Mesozoic, from 225 million years to 65 million years ago, is the time of the dinosaurs. It is divided into three periods, beginning with the Triassic. In the Triassic period, which began about 225 million years ago, the first dinosaurs appeared. Other creatures also evolved at this time, such as giant sea reptiles and small *mammals* (animals that keep a constant, warm body temperature and that feed their young with their own milk).

Dinosaurs ruled the land in the Jurassic period, from 193 million years to 135 million years ago. This is also the time when the first bird evolved. Dinosaurs were still plentiful until the end of the Cretaceous period, from 135 million to about 65 million years ago. At that time, the dinosaurs and most of the reptiles suddenly died.

The most recent era in Earth history is called the Cenozoic, which began 65 million years ago and continues today. This era is divided into two periods, the Tertiary and the Quaternary. In the Tertiary period, from 65 million to 2 million years ago, many types of mammals quickly began to appear. The first part of the Quaternary period, 2 million years ago, was marked by a great Ice Age in the

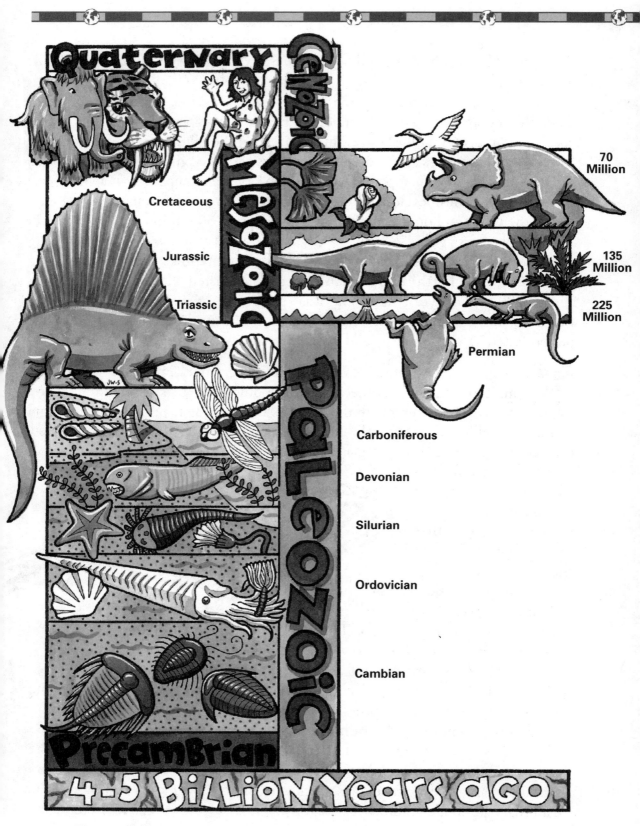

The timeline of Earth history, from the formation of the planet 4.5 billion years ago to the present period

Squeezing Earth History into One Year

It's hard to imagine the time span of Earth history when you talk about millions and billions of years. But if you compress the history of the planet into one year, the lengths of each era become clear.

In this calendar, 4,500 million years of Earth history have been turned into one year. The Pre-Cambrian Era takes up most of the calendar, running from January to mid-November. At the other end of the calendar, the Quaternary period, in which humans appeared on Earth, takes up only the last four hours of the last day of the year.

Northern Hemisphere, when giant sheets of ice blanketed much of North America, Europe, and Asia.

It is in the Quaternary period that humanlike beings called *hominids* appeared and then evolved into modern people like you and me. Human beings have only been around for the past 50,000 years. On a planet that is more than 4 billion years old, 50,000 years is a tiny sliver of time.

2

Go with the Flow

EARTH'S CRUST
ON THE MOVE

One Cozy Continent

Take a look at any world map. It's easy to imagine how some
of the continents could fit together like pieces of a
jigsaw puzzle. Notice how
the bulge on eastern South America fits into the
left side of Africa. The east coast of Greenland could
move west and connect to the islands of Canada. Saudi Arabia
would make a snug fit between Iran and the northeast coast of
Africa if the Persian Gulf and the Red Sea were not in the way.
Scientists have noticed the puzzle-piece shape of the continents for hundreds of years.

uropean explorers such as Christopher Columbus sailed to new continents in the fifteenth century. In the sixteenth century, mapmakers had enough information from the explorers to create world maps. One scientist who was interested in the shape and outline of the continents was the English philosopher-scientist Francis Bacon. He drew attention to the way the continents seemed to fit together in his book about science, *Novum Organum*, published in 1620.

Nonetheless it took a very long time for science to explain why some continents look as though they used to be connected to each other. In 1910, Robert Taylor suggested that the continents move. Taylor was an American **geologist** (a scientist who studies the history and structure of Earth) who was trying to understand how mountains were formed. He imagined that as the continents **collide**, they heap up at the edges just as a rug wrinkles if it slides across the floor. His **theory** (a scientific explanation) became known as **continental drift**.

Soon after Taylor announced his theory, scientists began to take a serious look at the subject of moving continents. At the center of the exciting search for answers was a German **meteorologist** (a scientist who studies weather and the atmosphere) named Alfred Wegener. He was fascinated with the shape of the continents, but some late-night reading about fossils really put him over the edge! He learned that scientists believed there was once a string of land connecting South America and Africa. This **land bridge** was the only way they could explain why fossils of the exact same kinds of animals were found in Africa and South America. The animals must have walked back and forth along the land bridge. Also, the same kind of garden snail found in western Europe was found in the eastern part of North America. This tiny creature could not have crossed the Atlantic Ocean.

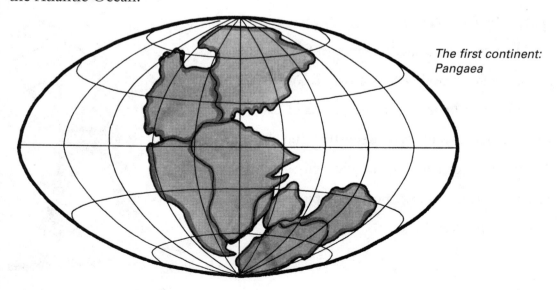

The first continent: Pangaea

These clues led Alfred Wegener to consider that long ago, all the continents were joined together as one big continent. He called this ancient supercontinent **Pangaea**. According to the fossil clues, he believed that Pangaea began breaking up about 200 million years ago, in the Mesozoic Era.

Breaking Up Is Hard to Do

If the continents were joined at one time, what caused them to break apart? Wegener thought the movement could have come from the tidal forces of the Moon and Sun. *Gravity* (the power of attraction between two objects) is the force that keeps objects, including people, held to the surface of Earth. The Moon attracts objects toward its surface, too—things from as far away as the surface of Earth. The Moon's gravity pulls on the oceans, gathering the water up and drawing it away from shorelines. The tide comes back in when the Moon's gravity weakens. The Sun's gravity also creates a pull on the surface of Earth, which affects the tides. Wegener thought that the power of gravity from our Moon and Sun could pull on continents, too, and make them slide from one place to another. He also thought that some of the power to move continents

The water in a boiling pot moves in a convection current. The same kind of current could move hot molten rock under Earth's crust.

EXPERIMENT

CONVECTION CURRENTS

Heat makes air and liquids, including molten rock, move. Using a piece of Styrofoam to represent a continent, this activity shows how convection currents make a surface object move.

What You Need:
- A clear glass bread pan

- Felt-tip marker

- Red food coloring

- 1 Styrofoam cup

- An adult helper

What to Do:
1. Ask an adult to help you cut off the bottom of the Styrofoam cup. Use a felt-tip marker to draw mountains and rivers on the flat, circular piece of Styrofoam to make it look like a minicontinent.
2. Fill the pan with water.
3. Ask an adult to help you at the stove.
4. Place one end of the pan over a small burner, and set the burner to the lowest setting.
5. Set the Styrofoam circle in the pan so that the circle floats on the water.
6. Add two drops of food coloring to the cool end of the pan.
7. Watch the pan from the side and the top.

What Happens and Why:
The colored water will move down and toward the warm end, then rise upward and back toward the cool end. This movement, which occurs in molten rock beneath Earth's surface, is a convection current. The current makes whatever is floating on the surface move around in the same way your Styrofoam circle moves.

came from the action of Earth spinning on its axis. The spinning motion of the planet, known as *centrifugal force*, would make some of Earth's outer layer fly off—or at least move. But many scientists thought that these forces were not strong enough to move continents. They believed that it would take much more power to move continents through hard rock.

Arthur Holms, a famous geologist from Scotland who admired Wegener's ideas, came up with a brilliant idea about the forces behind continental drift. He thought that heat inside Earth moved in pathways called **convection currents**. In the atmosphere, as well as in a pot of hot water, heat causes air and water to move in two directions. The hot air or water moves up, and the cooler air or water sinks down. Arthur Holms believed that there are convection currents inside Earth that push against the bottom of the crust, breaking and dragging it.

In 1928, there was no scientific evidence to support Holms's idea. However, his theory was proven years later with sensitive instruments that measured the temperature of Earth's crust beneath the oceans.

Deep-Sea Discoveries about Oceanic Crust

In the 1950s, new equipment using sound waves made amazing discoveries about the shape of the ocean floor. This new information led to a "deep-sea" understanding of how new crust is created on Earth, and what makes crust move.

Invisible Mountains: The Mid-Ocean Ridges

magine a mountain range longer than the Rockies, the Himalayas, and the Andes combined. A string of mountains this long would certainly be the dominant feature on the face of Earth. In the 1950s, the U.S. Navy discovered this 40,000-mile-long (64,400 km) mountain range—beneath the oceans!

Sonar: The "Eyes" of the Ocean

The first really detailed maps of the seafloor were made with the help of echo-sounding equipment called **sonar**. An echo sounder, carried on a ship, sends

HMS *Challenger:* First Explorer of the Ocean Depths

Oceanography, the study of the oceans, has led to many discoveries about the forces that move the continents. The official start of oceanography was marked on the day that a British ship called the HMS *Challenger* set sail for a trip around the world. The purpose of this ship's voyage from 1872 to 1876 was to gather information that would help lay telegraph cables. (The *telegraph,* an instrument that communicated by code over distances through a wire, was invented by Samuel Morse in 1844.) Among the many things the *Challenger* learned was that there seemed to be hills beneath the ocean. The ship measured the depth of the ocean by dropping measuring lines, with weights attached, to the bottom of the sea.

About 40 years later, new equipment would give scientists detailed information about the ocean floor. The maps created from these facts showed a seafloor full of amazing surprises.

sound waves down into the water. When the sound wave bounces back off of the ocean floor, the machine measures the distance the wave traveled. This measurement is possible because we know the speed at which sound moves through water. The length of time it takes for the echo wave to get back to the ship indicates the distance the wave has traveled. Once these distances are measured, a map can be drawn of the surface of the ocean floor.

Sonar was invented during World War I, and the first ship to use it for ocean study was the German ship *Meteor*. In search of gold deposits in the sea, the ship's echo sounder discovered a strange landscape beneath the water. Mountains rose higher than any others on Earth; huge, broad plains spread out the width of Kansas; and great valleys plunged deeper than the Grand Canyon.

Sonar technology had improved by the time U.S. Navy ships began crisscrossing the globe in the 1950s. Navy exploration revealed many details about the

EXPERIMENT

MAPPING THE OCEAN FLOOR

Using a few household objects to represent underwater mountains, this activity shows you how maps of the ocean floor were made.

What You Need:

- 2 matching chairs

- Scissors

- String

- Ruler

- Felt-tip marker

- 3 books of different sizes

- Small trash can

- Tissue box

- Washer

- Note paper

- Graph paper

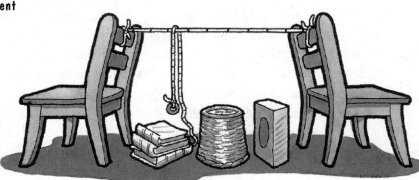

What to Do:

1. With the backs facing each other, place the chairs 3 feet (1 meter) apart.
2. Measure and cut the string into a 4-foot (1.2-m) section.
3. Tie the string to the top bar of each chair. Use enough string to tie each end so that there is exactly 3 feet (1 m) of stretched, taut string connecting the chairs.
4. Mark the string with the felt-tip marker at 3-inch (7.5-cm) intervals.
5. Place the objects in a line beneath the string: the stack of books, the upside-down trash can, and the tissue box set on its side (to make it tall).

continued

6. Measure and cut another piece of string that is 12 inches (30 cm) longer than the height of the chairs.
7. Tie one end of this string to the washer.
8. To create a measuring scale along this string, make a mark with the pen at every 1-inch (2.5-cm) interval.
9. Make two columns on a piece of note paper, one labeled "Distance from Shoreline," and the other "Depth Measurement."
10. Starting at the first 3-inch mark on one end of the string between the chairs, lower the scale until the washer touches the floor or an object.
11. Measure the depth at this point, using the marks on the scale and record it on your chart. If the measurement doesn't fall exactly on a scale marking, round off the measurement to the nearest marking.
12. Continue measuring and recording the data at every 3-inch interval of the surface string.
13. Using the data from your list, make a graph like the one in the illustration.

Distance from Shoreline	Depth Measurement
0 inch (0 cm)	33 inches (85 cm)
3 inches (7.5 cm)	33 inches (85 cm)
6 inches (15 cm)	29 inches (72.5 cm)
9 inches (22.5 cm)	29 inches (72.5 cm)
12 inches (30 cm)	29 inches (72.5 cm)
15 inches (37.5 cm)	0 inches (0 cm)
18 inches (45 cm)	26 inches (65 cm)
21 inches (52.5 cm)	26 inches (65 cm)
24 inches (60 cm)	0 inche (0 cm)
27 inches (67.5 cm)	24 inches (60 cm)
30 inches (75 cm)	24 inches (60 cm)
33 inches (82.5 cm)	0 inch (0 cm)
36 inches (90 cm)	0 inch (0 cm)

What Happens and Why:
Measuring the depth of the ocean floor along intervals used to be done with measuring lines like your piece of string and washer. Putting the mea-

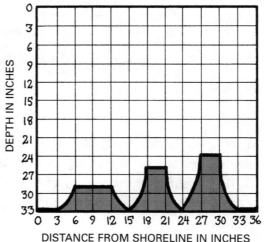

surements into a graph creates an image of the ocean floor, showing the different heights of mountains and other surface features.

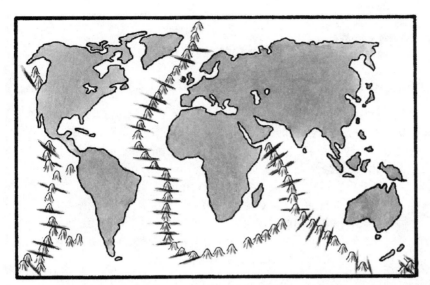

The mid-ocean ridges are a series of mountain ranges that extend over the entire Earth beneath the oceans.

mountains beneath the sea. Unlike the mountains above the sea on Earth, the undersea ridges are very sharp and jagged. They do not get smoothed down by wind and rain like the mountains out in the open air.

Today, a special type of sonar called the *SeaBeam system* is used to map the seafloor. SeaBeam sends out many sonar beams at once, making it possible to map whole sections of the seafloor in one pass. The information is put into a computer, which transforms it into a three-dimensional model of the mountains and trenches.

U.S. Navy sonar mapped the entire mountain range that snakes along the ocean floor of the planet. These **volcanic** (made from volcanoes) mountain

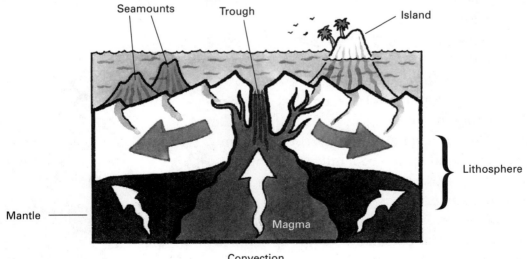

A mid-ocean ridge

The Tallest Mountain and the Deepest Valley

The tallest mountain in the world is in the ocean. Mauna Kea on the island of Hawaii, measured from its base on the seafloor, is 33,476 feet (10,043 m) high. Compare that to the highest peak on land, Mount Everest in the Himalayas, which rises 29,028 feet (8,848 m) high. The deepest trench, or valley, in the world also lies in the ocean. The Marianas Trench in the Pacific Ocean extends 36,198 feet (10,860 m) below the ocean floor. That's more than five times deeper than the Grand Canyon, which is only 7,000 feet (2,100 m) deep at its lowest point.

chains are formed along hot vents that spurt **lava** (molten rock that flows out to the surface of the land or the ocean floor). The mountain ranges beneath the oceans are called **mid-ocean ridges**.

The mountains of mid-ocean ridges can reach 2.5 miles (4 km) above the seafloor. Unlike mountains on the surface of Earth, which come to a point at the top, the mid-ocean ridges have a trough, or valley, along the top. This trough can be 7 to 9 miles (12–15 km) wide and 373 to 1,242 miles (600–2000 km) deep.

Every few hundred miles, a mid-ocean ridge is broken. The break is caused by the movement of Earth's crust. Hot lava flows up and breaks through the crust at the top of the mid-ocean ridges and then pours out. As it cools, it forms a new layer of crust.

As the current of hot rock flows outward on each side of a mid-ocean ridge, the crust spreads apart. This is called **seafloor spreading**. The seafloor is spreading apart at the rate of about 1/2 inch (1–2 cm) per year. The Pacific seafloor is spreading faster than the Atlantic seafloor. When a huge mass of lava rises up from a ridge, it can build up and cool into a tall mountain that goes above the surface of the water. This is how some islands in the oceans, such as Iceland in the north Atlantic, were created. Farther south in the Atlantic, a group of islands called the Azores were also created from volcanic activity. The Azores consist of nine islands that lie 760 miles (1,200 km) due west of Portugal. Volcanic islands in the Pacific are Tahiti, Easter Island, and the Hawaiian Islands.

Volcanoes that do not build up high enough to reach above the water are called **seamounts**. Some seamounts are flat on the top, as if the tip had been sliced off. These odd-looking seamounts, named **guyots**, were once volcanic mountains that rose above the surface of the water. As waves crashed over them, the top smoothed down and flattened. As the ocean crust spreads, guyots move away from the volcanic ridge on which they were formed.

The Rocky Recycling Program

Earth is not getting any bigger, even though lava is rising out of the seafloor and cooling to form new crust. Why isn't this new crust making Earth thicker? Far away from the mid-ocean ridges, near the edges of the continents, the ocean crust dips down and moves back into the mantle. As new crust rises up from the mid-ocean ridges, the same amount of old crust moves back down into the mantle. The movement of old crust back down into Earth is called **subduction**. In the hot mantle, the old crust breaks apart. Some of it will return to the surface millions of years later as lava flowing out of a mid-ocean ridge or a volcano. In this major recycling program, Earth's crust is replaced about every 200 million years.

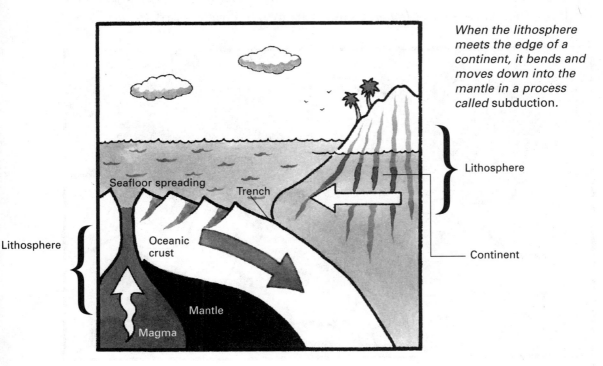

When the lithosphere meets the edge of a continent, it bends and moves down into the mantle in a process called subduction.

The Birth of an Island

The chain of islands that makes up Hawaii is still growing. A new volcano called Loihi is erupting just south of the island of Hawaii. Already 16,000 feet (4,800 m) high, Loihi needs to grow by another 3,000 feet (900 m) before it appears above water. Scientists predict this will take about 10,000 years. In 1963, a new island sprang up in the Atlantic just off the coast of Iceland.

This island, named Surtsey, was created in the same way as Iceland itself—from a volcano erupting in the mid-Atlantic ridge.

Plate Tectonics

Earth's lithosphere is broken up into sections called *plates*. The six major plates covering Earth are called the American, Eurasian, African, Indian, Antarctican, and Pacific. They are named after the continents or oceans that sit on them. These plates are also broken up into smaller plates. The movement of the plates is called **plate tectonics**. (*Tectonics* comes from the Greek word *teckton*, which

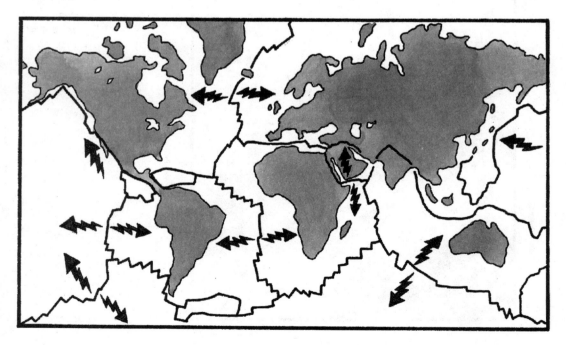

Six major plates make up the surface of Earth.

means "to build up and break down.") Plate tectonics is a better term than continental drift to describe the movement of Earth's crust. The movement of the plates is what causes the continents to drift along on top of them.

Plates have three different types of edges, or boundaries: (1) those at the mid-ocean ridges, where the new plates are being formed out of cooling lava; (2) those at trenches, where subduction takes place; and (3) those at cracks, or fractures, where plates are sliding past each other. When two plates meet at a fracture, they push against each other. This builds up **pressure**, which can only be released by the plates sliding along the fault. Put your hands together and rub them as if they're cold and you want to warm them up. Your hands slide against each other just like two plates move along a fracture.

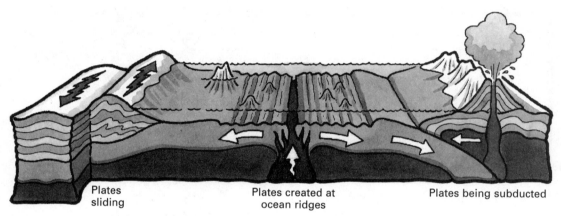

Plates sliding

Plates created at ocean ridges

Plates being subducted

Plates have three types of margins, or boundaries.

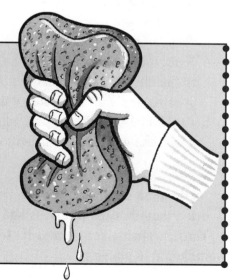

Rock Solid (Sort Of)

If the mantle is solid, how does lava flow through it? Mantle rock is full of tiny holes, just like a sponge. Pushed by the pressure inside Earth, lava seeps through these holes and flows up to the surface.

EXPERIMENT

CREATE SOME PLATES

In this activity, you'll make a slab that breaks up into sections like the plates of Earth.

What You Need:
- 2 cups (480 ml) of soil

- Water

- Plastic mixing bowl

- Cookie sheet with sides

What to Do:
1. Put the soil in the bowl and add $\frac{1}{2}$ cup (120 ml) water.
2. Stir the mixture, adding a little bit more water if needed, until the soil and water turn into thick mud.
3. Spread the mud onto the cookie sheet in an even layer. The layer should reach just below the top edge around the sides of the sheet.
4. Set the cookie sheet out in the sunshine for three days. (Bring it inside if it rains and wait for a sunny day.)
5. At the end of the third day, push down along the edges of the dried mud.

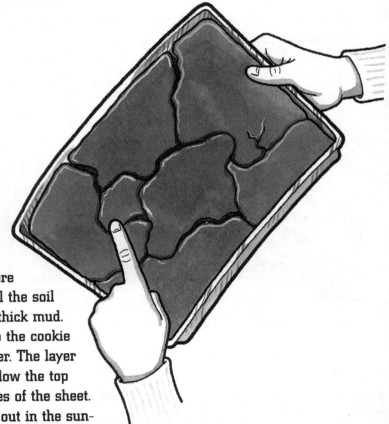

What Happens and Why:
As the mud dried, some of the water evaporated, and the mixture shrank. The dried mud cracked in places and broke into pieces that fit next to each other. These broken pieces represent the cracked surface of Earth's crust, which is broken into plates.

The Ride That Never Ends

The ancient supercontinent, Pangaea, wasn't the first land mass on Earth. It was created by the joining together of four smaller continents. **Huge** mountain ranges formed where these continents collided to become Pangaea. Fragments of these mountains still exist. One range is now spread out over several continents, and it includes the northern Appalachians in the United States; the mountains of eastern Greenland, western Ireland, and Scotland; and the highlands of Scandinavia. The other range formed on Pangaea is now called the Ural Mountain range, which extends 1,500 miles (2,414 km) north to south through western Russia. The lithosphere has always been on the move.

   This slow but steady movement will make Earth look very different 50 million years from now. Sea spreading in the Red Sea will push the Arabian peninsula away from Africa. Spreading at the mid-Indian ridge will push Australia north, and spreading in the Atlantic will push North and South America north and west.

Rocky Proof

Although many scientists liked the theory of continental drift, there was no real proof of it for hundreds of years. Rock-solid proof that the lithosphere is moving wasn't discovered until the late 1950s, when geologists learned something surprising about the ocean crust. The rock that makes up ocean crust is formed from molten material. As molten rock cools, it becomes slightly magnetized. The magnetic material within the rock reacts to the magnetic poles of Earth. As you found out in chapter 1, the north magnetic pole of Earth currently acts like the south pole of a magnet. This is the makeup of Earth's polarity. In the past, however, the poles were reversed. The igneous rock keeps a record of the polarity of Earth at the time the rock was formed.

With the use of **magnetometers** (instruments that read the magnetic properties of rocks), geologists discovered a striped pattern in the ocean crust. Each stripe contains rock from a different polarity. The earliest stripes go back 76 million years. The oldest stripes lie farthest away from a mid-ocean ridge, where the rock was created. This proves that the crust has been slowly moving for millions of years.

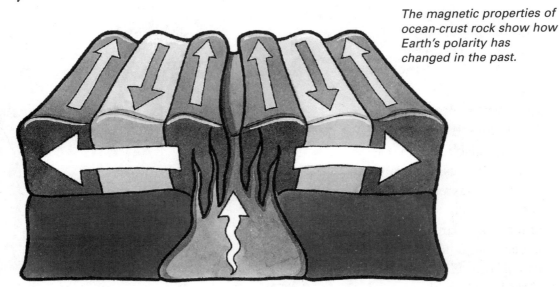

The magnetic properties of ocean-crust rock show how Earth's polarity has changed in the past.

Hydrothermal Vents, Giant Worms, and the Origins of Life

The molten rock beneath Earth's crust has another effect in addition to moving Earth's crust around and creating mountains. In some areas of the ocean where the crust is cracked from hot magma pressing up from beneath, cold seawater seeps down into the cracks, heats up, and spurts out again. This deep-sea hot spring is called a **hydrothermal vent**. The first hydrothermal vent was discovered in 1977 by the crew of *Alvin*, a submersible craft used to study the ocean depths.

Most of the deep ocean is too cold for plants or fish to live. But when *Alvin*'s headlights beamed on the ocean floor, 8,000 feet (2,400 m) below the Galapagos Islands in the Pacific Ocean, the crew saw an oasis teeming with life.

Hydrothermal vents made the water temperature comfortable for creatures no one had ever seen before. Giant red worms 6 feet (1.8 m) long stretched out of white tubes planted in the ocean floor. Palm worms, with a trunk and long tentacles that look like palm trees, waved in the hot current. Pure-white crabs wandered along the rocks looking for food. Some of the vents are called **black smokers** because they send out dark gases that look like smoke.

In addition to these animals, *Alvin* discovered a strange **microbe** (an organism too tiny to be seen without a microscope) that scientists believe is related to the very first forms of life that appeared billions of years ago. One of the greatest *mysteries* of science is the question of how life began in the boiling, poisonous mixture of liquids and gas that covered young Earth. Like the world's first organisms, the microbes found near ocean vents, called **archaea** ("ar-KEY-a"), live in temperatures just below the boiling point of water. They are able to use sulfur and other chemicals coming from the vents for energy. Other microbes need sunlight to create energy, but the archaea live in complete darkness.

3

Smash!

HOW TO BUILD

A MOUNTAIN

Some of the world's highest peaks, such as Mount Fuji in Japan and Mount Kilimanjaro in Africa, stand alone. These isolated mountains were once volcanoes built up from many layers of lava flowing out in a series of **eruptions**. But most mountains are arranged in long groups, strung together in giant ranges that stretch for thousands of miles. In South America, the Andes run 5,000 miles (8,045 km) along the west coast. The Himalayas in Asia stretch 1,500 miles (2,414 km) through northern India, Tibet, Nepal, Sikkim, and Bhutan. Unlike mountains formed by volcanoes, these mountain ranges were created when continents collided hundreds of millions of years ago.

World of Wonders

Colliding Plates— A Peak Experience

A mountain is made of layers of rock that have been folded and crumpled together. What force is strong enough to bend, tear, and push solid rock miles up into the air? Scientists have asked this question for centuries, but the mystery was not solved until plate tectonics explained how Earth's crust moves. The tectonic plates, which are always on the move, crash into each other and form mountains in two ways:

1. Head-on collisions of continents have thrown up ranges such as the Alps and the Himalayas.
2. When an ocean plate meets a continent, the plate plunges beneath it. Thick layers of ocean **sediment**, rocky material that has settled on the seafloor, is scraped off as the oceanic crust moves. The sediment heaps up onto the continent into a mountain range. The movement of the oceanic crust also causes the continental crust to crumple up. This type of collision, called **thrust faulting**, created the Andes and the Rockies. *Faulting* is the breaking and movement of layers of rock.

The Andes Mountains lie along the western edge of the South American continent, near the subduction area that created them. But the Rocky Mountains are

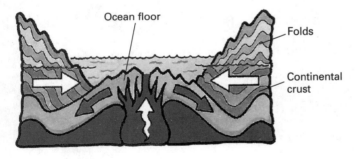

Ocean floor

Folds

Continental crust

a

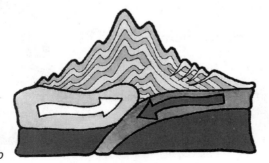

b

Mountain building from the collision of two plates:

(a) As two continents move toward each other over millions of years, they squeeze the ocean floor that separates them. As the oceanic crust is crushed and pushed deep into Earth, magma is created. The magma rises near the edges of each continent, pushing the continental crust up.

(b) As the plates continue to move together, the crust lifts, crumples, and folds, building a mountain range.

Major Mountains of the World

This list shows the highest peak on each major continent. More than 60 of the highest mountains in the world are found in the Himalayas and the nearby Karakoram range in Asia.

Mt. Everest	Mt. Aconcagua	Mt. McKinley	Kilimanjaro	Mt. Elbrus	Mt. Kosciusko
Asia	South America	North America	Africa	Europe	Australia
(Tibet)	(Argentina)	(Alaska)	(Tanzania)	(Russia)	(New South Wales)
29,028 feet	23,034 feet	20,320 feet	19,340 feet	18,510 feet	7,310 feet
(8,838 meters)	(7,021 meters)	(6,198 meters)	(5,894 meters)	(5,642 meters)	(2,228 meters)

hundreds of miles away from the west coast of the United States. Why are they so far away from the subduction zone? About 65 million years ago, the Rocky Mountains were formed where the Pacific plate collided with the North American plate. The Rocky Mountains rose up along the west coast, next to the Pacific Ocean, but since then, they have moved inland. As the Pacific plate continued to push against the North American plate, new mountains were made, and the Rocky Mountains were pushed eastward.

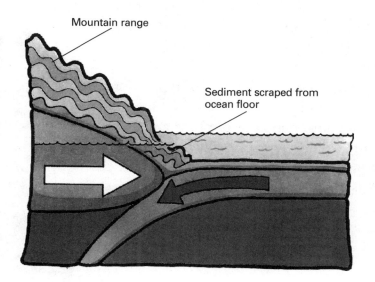

Mountain range

Sediment scraped from ocean floor

Continent

Mountain building from the subduction of a plate: When oceanic crust meets a continent, the crust plunges beneath it. Ocean sediment is scraped off and piles up on the continent, creating a mountain range.

The Dried-Up Apple Theory

In the mid-nineteenth century, geologists thought that mountains were made of folded rock, but they didn't know what caused the folding. Trekking over the Alps and other ranges, they observed distinct layers of rock piled into complex folds and shapes. James Dwight Dana (1813–1895), a geology professor at Yale University, came up with the idea that the mountains were formed by the cooling of Earth. Just as an apple's skin wrinkles as it dries, molten Earth shrank and crumpled in places as it cooled. If Dana's theory was correct, why didn't Earth wrinkle all over rather than in a few mountain ranges? The shrinking-Earth theory shriveled up and died as geologists made new discoveries about the continents and how they move. Earth is not shrinking or expanding, because new crust is being created at mid-ocean ridges and subducted at ocean trenches.

The Layered Look

The violent crushing and folding that creates a mountain range leaves the mountain surface lined with ridges. The rock that makes up the *foothills*, or lowest section of a mountain range, is sedimentary rock. This type of rock is created over millions of years, as bits of rock carried away by the wind fall and settle in layers. As each layer piles up over another, the layers squeeze together and harden.

The rock above the foothills is a complex mix of types. Some of the rock is igneous, such as granite, basalt, dolerite, and gabbro. During the birth of a mountain range, the pressure and heat acting upon the rock can make one type of rock change into a new type of rock. This process is called *metamorphism*, and the type of rock that results is called *metamorphic rock*. The molecular structure of limestone is **metamorphosed** into a pure white marble during mountain building. Other types of metamorphic rock found in mountains are mica, slate, phyllite,

YOU CAN MOVE MOUNTAINS!

With some modeling clay and a couple of wooden blocks, you and a friend can mimic the way rocks fold into mountains when continents collide.

What You Need:
- Modeling clay in at least two different colors

- 2 wood blocks, about 2" (5 cm) high and 5" (13 cm) wide

What to Do:
1. Form the modeling clay into four strips about 18" long.
2. On a table, place the strips on top of one another, alternating the colors to represent layers of rock.
3. Place a block at each end of the layered clay strips. Ask a friend to act as a "continent" with one of the blocks.
4. Slowly push the blocks together at the same time.

What Happens and Why:
As the blocks move together, the strips of clay fold and bunch up. The longer the strips of clay, the more complex your series of folds. This is what happens to layers of rock as they are squeezed by two continents moving together.

kyanite, and gneiss. Mountains contain an amazing variety of rocks that have gone through many changes.

A Mountain's Changing Face

The peaks of the Alps and Himalayas are sharp and broken because they reach into heights where the temperature often dips below freezing. In these cold temperatures, high mountains are damaged by ice. Water expands when it freezes and turns to ice. When rainwater seeps into a mountain crack and freezes, it expands with a powerful force that breaks the rock apart. Huge areas of broken mountain rock that has been shattered by ice are called **screes.**

The Appalachians, which are older than the Alps and the Himalayas, have been worn down through a process called **weathering** (the breakdown of rock when it is exposed to rain, air, and sun). Towering and majestic when they were created hundreds of millions of years ago, the Appalachians have been beaten down by wind and rain that tears away at the surface. Weathering also occurs when chemical reactions between the air and the rock dissolve the rock. Chemical weathering occurs when raindrops pick up acid substances in the air. When the acid-containing raindrop falls on rock, the acid eats away at the rock.

They're Still Growing

We live in a mountain-building age. Mount Everest in the Himalayas is growing about 0.4 inches (1 cm) taller every year. Two other mountain ranges that are still growing—but at a very slow rate—are the Alps in Europe and the Andes in South America.

The Alps were created when the African plate slammed into the bottom of the Eurasian plate (Europe) 250 million years ago. The plates began drifting apart 200 million years ago, with the Mediterranean Sea filling up the space in between. About 40 million years ago, however, the African plate began to move north again. Since then, it has brought the continent of Africa 250 miles (400 km) closer to Europe. The impact of the African and Eurasian plates pressing together is bringing more *rumpling* and folding to the Alps.

The Pacific plate continues to move toward South America and to plunge beneath that continent. This is lifting more ocean sediment up into the Andes. Young sediment can be found high above sea level on the mountains, which shows that the uplift is happening at a quick pace.

4

All Stressed Out
THE STORY OF EARTHQUAKES

On October 17, 1989, I was in San Francisco for the World Series to do some interviews for *Good Morning America*. There was a game that day at Candlestick Park, but I was in my hotel room writing down the questions I wanted to ask some baseball players later in the day. It was a beautiful afternoon, and I had a great view of downtown San Francisco from my nineteenth-floor window. Suddenly the building started shaking from side to side and jumping **Up** and **down!** I thought it was the end of the world! A roar like a freight train filled the room, and for about three seconds I froze in my tracks, sure that the whole building was going to fall apart. Rather than wait for the hotel to crash on my head, I ran out of my room and raced down the staircase. The steel beams inside the walls were **creaking**, and the horrible roaring sound echoed through the stairwell. After I'd gone down only two flights, the shaking stopped. It had lasted only 15 to 18 seconds, but it seemed like forever!

The earthquake I experienced in San Francisco killed 67 people, injured 3,000 more, and damaged or destroyed more than 100,000 buildings. It caused a 30-foot (9 m) section of the Bay Bridge, which connects Oakland to San Francisco, to collapse. The bridge looked like a wafer cookie that had been snapped into pieces.

Early Explanations

The ancient Greeks thought that earthquakes occurred when Atlas, the god who held Earth on his shoulders, shrugged. The Tzotzil Indians of southern Mexico believed Earth shook when a giant jaguar brushed up against the pillars of the world. In ancient Japanese tradition, earthquakes were caused by the flopping around of a giant catfish that lived inside Earth. And in Europe in the eighteenth century, the pope declared that earthquakes were God's punishment for humanity's lack of faith in God.

Why the Earth Quakes

The theory of plate tectonics that we learned about in chapter 2 explains why most earthquakes occur. Earthquakes and volcanoes are created at the edge of the plates, where oceanic crust sinks into trenches or where two plates meet and grind against each other. More than a million earthquakes occur every year, but many are tiny **tremors** (shaking movements) that are too small to be felt.

Ninety percent of all earthquakes occur around the border of the vast Pacific plate. There is so much earthquake and volcanic activity on the edges of this plate that the outline is called the **Ring of Fire**. The west side of the Pacific plate is plunging beneath the Eurasian plate and the Indo-Australian plate, causing a stretch of earthquake activity from New Zealand to Japan. The east side of the Pacific plate is **sliding** northward against the North American plate at the rate of about 2 inches (5 cm) per year. South of California all the way down the Pacific coast of South America, the Nazca plate is being pushed beneath the South American plate, creating a long line of earthquakes along the Ring of Fire.

Ninety percent of the world's earthquakes occur along the Ring of Fire.

The next largest area of earthquake activity is in the Alpide belt, which extends from the Mediterranean region eastward through Turkey, Iran, and northern India. Although only 5 to 6 percent of all earthquakes occur here, the many large cities in the zone are devastated when an earthquake hits.

Earthquakes at Ocean Trenches

When oceanic crust bends and dips below a continental plate, it moves in sudden, jerky movements. The moving oceanic crust presses against the continental plate, creating pressure. When the rock can't bear the stress any longer, the oceanic crust jerks downward. This sudden movement releases an earthquake—a huge amount of energy blasting out in all directions in the form of seismic waves. **Seismology** is the term for the science of earthquakes, and scientists who study earthquakes are called seismologists. The spot below the ground where the earthquake occurs is called the **focus**. The point on the surface directly above the focus is called the **epicenter**. The focus of most earthquakes is considered shallow if it is less than 44 miles (70 km) below the surface. Deep-focus earthquakes extend from 186 miles to 435 miles (300 km to 700 km) underground. Shallow earthquakes bring more damage because the seismic waves do not have far to travel before reaching the surface.

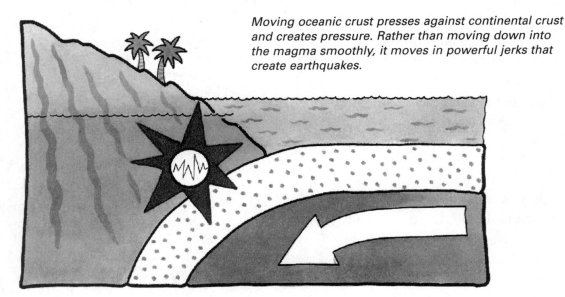

Moving oceanic crust presses against continental crust and creates pressure. Rather than moving down into the magma smoothly, it moves in powerful jerks that create earthquakes.

Earthquakes at Fault Lines

When there is no trench at the edge of a continent, oceanic crust crashes into continental crust and slides along it. This crashing breaks up rock along the edges of both plates. The area of broken, unstable rock along the edges of a plate is called a **fault**. Sometimes the movement of a fault causes the surface of the ground to crack. But not all faults lie close to the surface.

The most famous and most closely studied fault in the world is the **San Andreas Fault** that runs along most of western California. Here, the Pacific plate is scraping against the North American plate. The fault area is 60 miles (111 km) wide and 800 miles (1,482 km) long and extends 10 miles (19 km) into the ground. There have been more than 20 major earthquakes along this fault in the past 90 years.

Pressure builds up as the Pacific and North American plates grind against each other. If the plates move slowly, continuously releasing pressure, the movement is called **fault creep.** Fault creep can break drainpipes lying in the ground, shift streambeds, and make doors jam in their frames. Though annoying, such events are not usually devastating. In contrast, when the plates stick together and build up pressure over time, the sudden release of that pressure creates a major earthquake.

San Francisco lies directly on the San Andreas Fault. In 1906, this bustling western city was jolted by one of the biggest earthquakes in history. Even during major earthquakes, the plates do not usually move more than a few inches or a few feet. During the 1906 San Francisco earthquake, however, the plates shifted 22 feet (6.7 m)! Some people believe that the quakes that have occurred since 1906 have not released all the pressure building up at the San Andreas Fault. They predict that the "Big One" could happen at any time.

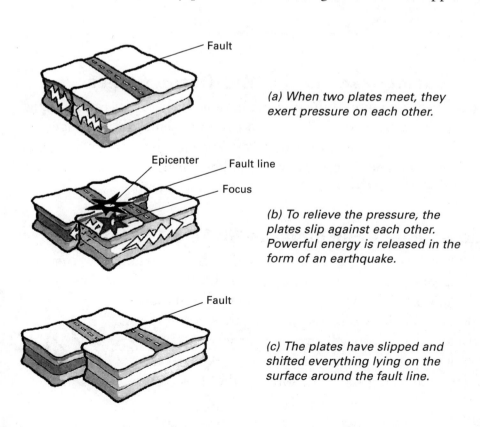

Fault

(a) When two plates meet, they exert pressure on each other.

Epicenter   Fault line

Focus

(b) To relieve the pressure, the plates slip against each other. Powerful energy is released in the form of an earthquake.

Fault

(c) The plates have slipped and shifted everything lying on the surface around the fault line.

The Pacific plate slips against the North American plate at the San Andreas Fault in California.

Earthquakes in the Mid-Ocean Ridges

Plate boundaries are found at the mid-ocean ridges, where new crust is being created. As the crust is pushed outward from the center of the ridge, the pressure on the rock creates earthquakes. Fortunately, these earthquakes occur far away from land and do not damage buildings or people. However, they can cause huge tidal waves that can do a lot of damage.

Tsunami: When Earthquakes Make a Big Splash

Earthquakes that occur under the ocean can cause huge waves known as *tsunamis* or *tidal waves*. But these waves have nothing to do with the tide. Tsunamis hit Alaska, Hawaii, Portugal, and other places, but most of them strike Japan because of the many earthquakes that occur beneath the ocean near Japan. When the crust jerks suddenly beneath the ocean, the powerful movement creates a wave in the water. The force of the

A Crack in the Theory

Plate tectonics gives a clear explanation why earthquakes occur. It makes a lot of sense that an earthquake—an explosion of energy—is released when whole sections of the earth's crust slip against each other. But why do earthquakes occur in areas that are nowhere near the edges of plates? In 1811, a violent earthquake shook Missouri, in the heart of the North American continent. One of the most devastating earthquakes in the history books hit Lisbon, Portugal, in 1755. Records reveal that this earthquake was so powerful it was felt in southern France and northern Africa. Curiously, Lisbon does not lie near a plate boundary. Great Britain, which also lies far away from a plate boundary, has more than 120 earthquakes every 100 years. A moderate quake hit Britain in 1990, and the worst British quake on record occurred in 1884, destroying every building in a village in Essex and causing bizarre events in the Houses of Parliament in London. Members of Parliament were suddenly thrown against walls, and papers and briefcases flew from their hands.

Earthquakes have jolted almost every part of the world. Scientists don't know why they occur in places that should be free of violent plate movement. For now, it's a mystery. But one day, an imaginative young scientist like you may come up with a new theory that explains it!

earthquake in deep water can create a tsunami up to 35 feet (11 m) high, and these **giant** waves move at incredible speeds. In 30,000 feet (9,144 m) of water, a tsunami can speed along at 670 miles per hour (1,240 km/h). In 3,000 feet (914 m), it moves more slowly at 212 miles per hour (393 km/h)—but that's still fast enough to do a lot of damage when it hits land.

When an earthquake occurs in the ocean far from land, seismologists can warn residents in coastal areas of an approaching tsunami. But when an earthquake happens near the shore, there isn't time for a warning. On July 12, 1993, a major earthquake struck off the coast of Hokkaido, the northernmost island of Japan. In less than five minutes, this very powerful quake caused a 100-foot-high tsunami to crash ashore, killing 180 people.

Seismic Waves

The violent shaking I felt in my hotel during the 1989 San Francisco earthquake came from three types of shock waves. Two of these waves are called **body waves** because they travel underground. The fastest body waves are **primary waves**, or **P waves**. Moving about 4 miles per second (6.4 km/second), P waves are the first shocks felt when an earthquake occurs. They flow out from the focus, racing through solid rock and softer materials within the earth. Rock is stretched and **squeezed** as P waves pass through it. When these waves reach the surface, they make the ground bounce up and down. The strange booming and thundering sound I heard during the earthquake was

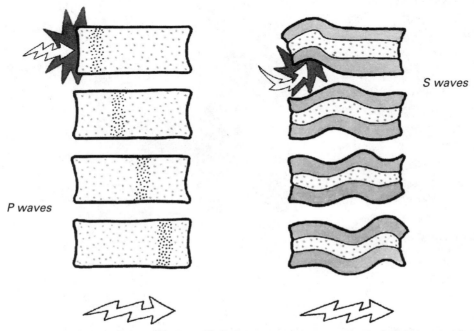

P waves

S waves

caused by P waves. Passing through rock in the same way sound waves flow through the air, P waves create a **booming** and thundering sound when they hit the surface.

Secondary, or **S waves**, are body waves that travel about half as fast as P waves. S waves travel through rock in a side-to-side motion and make the ground move both side-to-side and up-and-down.

Body waves shake and rattle the ground even more when their energy is reflected back into the ground. When they hit the surface, they bounce back into the earth and create **surface amplification**. This makes the shaking even worse because waves moving toward the surface join up with waves on the way down. More waves means more movement of the ground.

Surface waves, the third type of shock waves that come with earthquakes, occur only on top of the ground. They move more slowly than P or S waves and are named after the scientists who defined them. **Love waves** shake the ground from side-to-side, and **Rayleigh waves** move the ground up-and-down and side-to-side. Rayleigh waves make the ground roll in a wavy motion, just like heavy waves at sea roll a boat (and make your stomach churn).

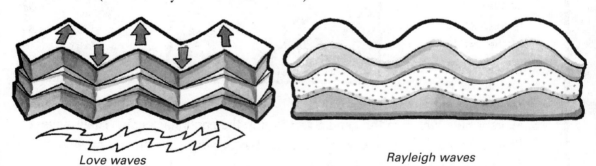

Love waves   Rayleigh waves

Measuring Earthquakes

Earthquakes are described in two ways: by **magnitude,** the power of an earthquake as recorded by a seismograph; and by **intensity,** a description of the physical damage caused by an earthquake. A seismograph writes squiggly lines that represent earthquake waves. Hanging weights called *pendulums,* hung within a frame, swing when the earth shakes. A pen hangs from each weight, with its point

SHOCK WAVES

In this experiment, you'll create invisible shock waves that are strong enough to blow out a candle.

What You Need:
- Empty round salt container
- Candle

What to Do:

1. Remove the metal spout from the salt container.
2. Ask an adult to light the candle for you.
3. Stand about 3 feet (1 m) away from the candle, and aim the hole in the container at the candle.
4. Sharply thump the end of the container facing you with your finger.

5. Move a little closer to the candle and thump the container again. Then move a little farther away from where you started. How far away can you move and still send out a wave that blows out the candle?

What Happens and Why:

The thumping action creates a shock wave in the air, which flows in the direction of the candle, making the flame move. Shock waves that flow through Earth are also invisible but have an effect on the things they contact. The shock wave can also be called a *sound wave*. When the shock wave hit your eardrums, it moved them just as it moved the candle flame, causing you to hear the thumping sound.

touching paper that rolls beneath the pens. As the weights move, the pens record the movement on the paper. Pendulums that bob up and down record the vertical (up-and-down) motion of Earth, and pendulums that move from side to side record horizontal motion. The bigger the motion of Earth, the bigger the movement of the pendulum, and the wider the wiggle of the line on the paper.

Modern seismographs read the pendulum movement and change it into an electric code. The code, or electric signal, moves through telephone wires or through the air as radio waves. The signal is sent to a moving needle called a *stylus*, which records the wave on either paper or magnetic tape. Most of today's seismographs are placed in deep holes underground or in the countryside, where the vibrations of cars and airplanes cannot mix in with earthquake waves. In 1931, there were 350 seismograph stations around the world. Today there are more than 4,000 stations that communicate with each other through computer and satellite linkups. This increase in seismographic information allows more quakes to be detected now than in earlier years.

A seismograph that records the horizontal motion of Earth

Seismographs in different locations are used to find the epicenter of an earthquake. Three or more seismograph stations use their wave measurements to find out how far away they are from the epicenter.

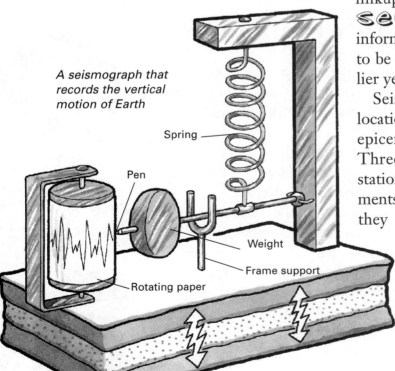

A seismograph that records the vertical motion of Earth

Three or more seismograph stations map the location of an earthquake's epicenter.

If the readings tell a seismologist that her or his station is 50 miles from the epicenter, the seismologist draws a circle on a map that extends 50 miles out in every direction from the station. The circles from all the stations are then put onto one map. The point where they all overlap is the epicenter of the quake.

The Richter Scale

Whenever you hear the report of an earthquake, it's described by a number on the **Richter scale**. Created by seismologist Charles Richter in 1935, the Richter scale shows the amount of energy released by an earthquake. Information from seismographs is used in a mathematical formula to give an earthquake a number greater than 0 and less than 9 according to Richter's original scales. Each leap to a higher number increases the **magnitude** by 10. An earthquake measuring 5 on the Richter scale is 10 times stronger than one measuring 4, and 100 times stronger than one measuring 3. Most earthquakes that are reported measure between 3 and 8.

Look out! The Dragon Just Fed the Frog!

The world's first instrument for recording earthquakes was invented in China in the second century A.D. Created by the astronomer and geographer Chang Heng, this big device, which we now call a *seismoscope*, was made out of bronze and measured about 6 feet (2 m) in diameter. Inside hung a pendulum that would swing from the movement of a tremor too weak to be felt by a person. Attached to the pendulum were bars connected to a series of dragon head sculptures on the outside of the vessel. When the pendulum swung, it pulled on one of the bars. The bar opened the mouth of the dragon head attached to it.

A bronze ball was released from the dragon's mouth and fell with a clang into the open mouth of a frog sculpture sitting at the base of the vessel. This seismoscope recorded the movement of an earthquake, as well as showing from which direction the earthquake came.

In A.D. 138, Chang Heng used his invention to announce that a major earthquake had struck 400 miles northwest of Loyan, the Chinese capital. His report came long before messengers on horseback brought news of the earthquake to the capital city.

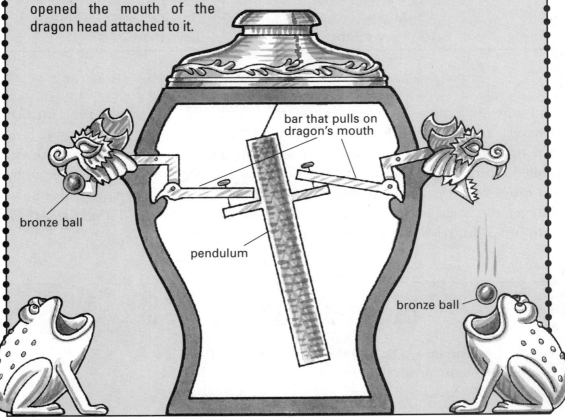

bar that pulls on dragon's mouth

bronze ball

pendulum

bronze ball

The formula used to turn seismograph readings into Richter-scale numbers does not work well for very strong earthquakes. Since Richter invented the scale in 1935, more precise seismograph readings have been taken. To make a more accurate magnitude measurement of **powerful** quakes, seismologists updated the magnitude scale in 1977. They went back to read seismograph information from quakes classified as "great" and to revise the magnitude rating. For example, a great quake that struck Alaska in 1964 had been rated magnitude 8.4. After being rechecked, the rating was changed to 9.2. This shows that the earthquake was almost 10 times stronger than previously believed!

THE RICHTER MAGNITUDE SCALE

Earthquake Type	Magnitude
Great	8 and up
Major	7 to 7.9
Strong	6 to 6.9
Moderate	5 to 5.9
Light	4 to 4.9
Minor	3 to 3.9
Very minor	Less than 3

Large earthquakes almost always strike within a cluster of many smaller quakes. The largest quake is called the **mainshock**, any quakes that occur before the mainshock are called **foreshocks**, and quakes hitting after the mainshock are called **aftershocks**. Within the first hour of an earthquake that is large enough to cause damage, many aftershocks that can be felt on the ground will follow. Bigger earthquakes have more and larger aftershocks. Some **tremors** can be felt for days after a major earthquake.

California Quakes

California is struck by a major earthquake (7.0 to 7.9 on the Richter scale) about once every 18 years.

John Milne, the Father of Modern Seismology

All seismographs work on Chang Heng's pendulum principle. In the 1800s, scientists experimented with different designs for recording earthquake waves. In 1856, the Italian scientist Luigi Palmieri (1807–1896) invented a device using pendulums, mercury-filled tubes, springs, and electricity. It was connected to a separate machine that recorded the movements on a tiny paper strip.

The seismometer invented by John Milne (1850–1913) contained all the parts to detect and measure waves in one neat unit. A *seismometer* detects the seismic waves, a *seismograph* makes a visible record of it, and a *seismogram* is the term for the written record. Although Milne was born in England, he did most of his important work in Japan, where he lived and taught for many years. Milne's device contained three pendulums, three pens to trace vertical shaking and two directions of horizontal shaking, and a clock to indicate when a quake starts. Modern seismographs still use pendulums and metal pens called *styluses* to record seismic waves. Milne set up the Seismological Society of Japan to study earthquakes. When he retired from teaching, he and his Japanese wife moved to England. From his house, he set up the first network to collect information from seismographs all over the world.

"Did You Feel That?" Measuring How Earthquakes Feel and the Damage They Do

Richter-scale numbers give a scientific measurement of an earthquake. But they don't say anything about what the quake does to buildings and people. The intensity of an earthquake describes how an earthquake affects things. An earthquake has only one Richter magnitude, but it has many intensities. The intensity at the epicenter is much greater than the intensity 100 miles away. In 1902, the Italian scientist Giuseppe Mercalli (1850–1914) created a method of describing earthquakes by the effect they have on things. To avoid confusion with

Richter-scale numbers, the Mercalli scale uses Roman numerals. This scale was updated in 1931 with more detailed descriptions.

Even though they aren't scientific, intensity scales are important. Physical descriptions of earthquake damage were the only records available about earthquakes that occurred before the invention of seismographs and the Richter scale. Using these descriptions, seismologists have made estimates of major earthquakes in history.

The Modified Mercalli Intensity Scale

I. Shaking is recorded by instruments but is not felt by people.

II. Only people at rest, especially in the upper floors of buildings, feel shaking.

III. People indoors feel it as a slight vibration. Cars that aren't moving may rock slightly.

IV. People both inside and outdoors can feel it. If the quake occurs at night, some people are awakened. Dishes rattle, wooden walls creak, parked cars rock noticeably.

V. Nearly everyone feels it. Liquid in glasses splashes out, small objects knock over, doors swing open and close.

VI. Everyone feels it. Many people are frightened and rush outdoors. People walk unsteadily, windows and dishes break, pictures fall off walls.

VII. It is difficult to stand. Furniture breaks, loose bricks and plaster fall, waves appear on ponds, large bells ring.

VIII. Driving is difficult. Walls, chimneys, steeples, and statues fall. Tree branches break, the flow of wells and springs changes, and cracks appear in wet ground.

IX. General panic arises. Animals run around in confusion. Underground pipes break, foundations of buildings are damaged, and frame buildings shift off their foundations.

X. Most brick and frame buildings are destroyed. Some well-built wooden buildings are destroyed. Water is thrown out of rivers. Large landslides occur.

XI. Railroad rails bend greatly, underground pipes go out of service, and highways become useless. Large cracks appear in the ground, and landslides and rockfalls occur.

XII. Total damage occurs to all structures above and below ground. Waves are seen on the ground surface. Objects are thrown into the air. River courses are moved.

Bizarre Things Animals Do before an Earthquake

- Rats seem to panic and are unafraid of people.

- Horses refuse to eat or enter the barn.

- Birds stay away from trees.

- Cockroaches scramble around as if they can't decide where to go.

- Pet goldfish swim around frantically.

- Freshwater fish jump up wildly in lakes and ponds.

- Deer and rabbits run away from the future epicenter of a quake.

Animals are more sensitive to vibrations, magnetic fields, electricity, and odors than humans. This may explain why they act so strangely before an earthquake.

Can Earthquakes Be Predicted? Ask a Cockroach or a Snake

Earthquakes are violent, destructive—and unpredictable! The overall history of earthquakes leads to one general rule: The more time that has passed since an earthquake, the bigger the chance one will strike. Seismologists use information about past earthquakes to guess probabilities about future earthquakes. *Probability* shows the likelihood that something will happen, but it is not a prediction. Within the next 30 years, there is a 60-percent probability that an earthquake will hit somewhere in southern California. But exactly where or when is a mystery.

In at least one case, an earthquake has been **predicted** by paying attention to clues from nature. In China, strange events that often happen before an earthquake are used as clues to forecasting a quake. Quakes have been studied for nearly 4,000 years in China, and there are records of more than 9,000 earthquakes going back to the year 1831 B.C. The official earthquake records of the state of California only go back to 1930!

In their long, hard look at earthquakes, the Chinese have observed many things. Before an earthquake, animals act in bizarre ways, the ground changes shape, and Earth's **magnetic** field gets stronger in the earthquake area. The water in wells bubbles up and then returns to its normal level. As the first seismic waves flow through underground rock, they shake up gases that can enter underground water supplies, giving the water a bitter taste. Also, a series of small earthquakes can mean that a big quake is on its way.

The Chinese used these clues in 1974 to make the first successful prediction of an earthquake. In early 1974, seismologists recorded many minor quakes occurring in the Liaoning province in Manchuria. Quakes had not occurred there for 100 years. They noticed that the land had become strangely uplifted and tilted, and Earth's magnetic field was growing stronger in the area. On December 22, after another burst of small tremors, the State Seismological Bureau in Beijing forecasted that an earthquake of magnitude 5.5–6 could be expected near the town of Yingkou within six months.

All through that section of the province, animals started to **act strangely**. Snakes that had been hibernating for the winter awoke, slithered out of their hiding places, and lay frozen on the snowy surface. Small pigs ran around and chewed off each other's tails. Rats ran around in the open, too agitated to fear humans.

In February 1975, 500 small tremors shook through the Yingkou area within 72 hours. The biggest of them hit on the morning of February 4—then all was quiet. City leaders immediately ordered all 3 million residents of the town to leave their homes and put up straw shelters and tents far away from buildings. Even though the temperature was below freezing, the Chinese people obeyed. It was a smart move because at 7:36 that evening, a major earthquake struck. Roads and bridges broke apart, the earth rolled up and down, and most of the buildings in Yingkou were destroyed.

Three hundred people died in the quake, but tens of thousands more would have died if they had not moved to safety.

The United States Geological Survey, which studies earthquakes and volcanoes, has never predicted a major earthquake. But seismologists in the United States and throughout the world are studying nature's earthquake signals. Seismic waves affect the magnetic property of rocks, the shape of the land, and the chemical makeup of water. When instruments are invented that can closely detect these changes, we will be on our way to predicting earthquakes.

5

Mountains of Fire
VOLCANOES INSIDE AND OUT

It's hard to believe, but **volcanoes**, spurting out melted rock from deep within the earth, are the source of all life on the planet. Important gases in the air you breathe were created by volcanic eruptions billions of years ago. The ground you walk on is partly an ancient layer of **molten rock** from volcanoes that hardened as the rock cooled. All the water on Earth began as steam from volcanoes, which formed clouds and fell to Earth as rain, filling the oceans. Much of the soil in which things grow is created from volcanic ash rich in minerals. Without the atmosphere, continents, water, or soil, you would not be here!

Earth is still cooling, and with each passing century, volcanic activity slows down. Millions of years from now, Earth will be as cold and quiet as the Moon, which cooled more quickly because it is smaller than Earth. But for now, about 500 active volcanoes still dot the planet's surface.

How a Volcano Is Born

People have noticed for thousands of years that where there are volcanoes, there are earthquakes. Modern science explains this relationship with plate tectonics. There are three places where volcanoes form. Most are found in long, narrow bands where the earth's crust is diving beneath another plate of crust. Two thirds of the world's active volcanoes are found in the Ring of Fire, which surrounds the Pacific plate. Some are found beneath the sea, where new crust is being made at mid-ocean ridges. Earthquakes are also created at both of these places, as shown in chapter 4. A third type of volcano is formed over a hot spot, a long tube of magma that is rooted deep in the earth.

Not all volcanoes look like tall, smooth mountains. Anywhere that lava flows from an opening in the earth is a volcano, even if it's just a hole in the crust. The opening through which volcanic materials come to the surface is called a **vent**.

Volcanoes Formed at Plate Boundaries

Like the other islands of Japan, Mount Fuji is one of the volcanoes formed as the Pacific plate plunges beneath the Eurasian plate. As the oceanic crust moves into the earth, it heats up. Just 25 miles below the surface, the temperature is 1,600° Fahrenheit (870° Celsius), and the rock is white-hot. A piece of metal would melt long before it got this hot. When it reaches the mantle, oceanic crust melts and becomes molten rock (magma). Because oceanic crust is made out of lighter rock than continental crust, the melted oceanic rock rises through the heavier rock surrounding it. The magma gathers together in an underground pool called a **magma chamber**. Water and gases are also found inside Earth's crust. They mix with the magma in the magma chamber. At the top of the chamber, the magma mixture is carried toward the surface through a narrow tunnel called a **feeder pipe**.

Remember, the pressure inside Earth is stronger the deeper you go. Rising up to areas of less and less pressure, the bits of magma spread apart. Finally, just like a can of soda that's been shaken up, the top is blown in a huge explosion. The volcano **erupts** with more power than a nuclear bomb, blasting a hole through the surface of the volcano. Bright red lava shoots into the sky, cooling and becoming solid as soon as it hits the air. Lava that cools into bits of dust is called **ash.** Lava that hardens into very lightweight rocks and boulders is called **pumice.** The water from the magma chamber shoots up as steam, building a giant cloud over the volcano. Ash and pumice pile up in layers around the fountain of lava, giving it a cone shape. With each eruption, the volcano builds up thicker slopes from new layers of lava and can grow to great heights.

Lava can shoot out from a volcano for two days during a violent eruption. The magma chamber, which may have been growing for hundreds of thousands of years, empties out completely. When the eruption is over, the volcano is quiet.

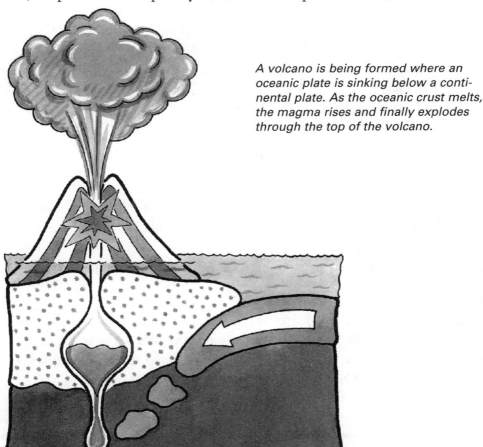

A volcano is being formed where an oceanic plate is sinking below a continental plate. As the oceanic crust melts, the magma rises and finally explodes through the top of the volcano.

EXPERIMENT

BUILD YOUR OWN ERUPTING VOLCANO!

What You Need:

- Funnel

- 16-ounce plastic soda bottle

- Baking soda

- Smaller plastic bottle

- Vinegar

- Red food coloring

- Cake pan or baking dish

- Soil and sand

What to Do:

1. Place the funnel in the mouth of the soda bottle, and pour in baking soda until the bottle is half full.
2. Fill the smaller bottle about half full of vinegar.
3. Add about 6 drops of food coloring to the vinegar.
4. Stand the soda bottle in the center of the pan, and pile soil and sand around it in the shape of a mountain. The mouth of the soda bottle should be showing on top, with the funnel resting in it.
5. Quickly pour the red vinegar into the soda bottle through the funnel.

What Happens and Why:

The vinegar reacts with the baking soda to form carbon-dioxide gas. The gas expands out of the bottle, just as the gases in magma cause it to erupt from a volcano. The red "lava" in this activity was carried to the surface through the opening in the soda bottle.

Beneath the ground, more oceanic crust is melting into magma at the same spot. New molten rock begins to rise into the magma chamber. One day, it will blast to the surface—and the volcano will blow its top again. When there is no more magma to fill up the chamber, the volcano will shrink. Over millions of years, wind and rain smooth the mountain down until the volcano's life cycle is over.

Mount St. Helens: Fireworks in April

Volcanoes that have violent eruptions between long periods of quiet are called **strato-volcanoes.** They form steep cone shapes. In 1980, the people of northwestern Washington experienced a strato-volcano eruption in all its fiery and deadly glory.

Mount St. Helens, a volcano in the Cascade Range, had been quiet for more than 100 years. Because it has erupted about every 100 to 150 years since the year 1400, an eruption wouldn't be a surprise. Any one of the Cascade volcanoes—such as Mount Rainier, Mount Shasta, and Mount Hood—could erupt at any time. Volcanoes that are inactive but are expected to erupt again in the future are **dormant volcanoes.** A volcano that is not active and is not expected to erupt again is an **extinct volcano.** The volcanoes of the Cascade Range are formed from the Pacific plate moving beneath the North American plate. As the Pacific plate crust melts, it rises up to form the volcanoes.

In March 1980, Mount St. Helens began to make rumbling noises. Deep rumblings and tremors are caused by earthquakes beneath volcanoes. The earthquakes occur as magma starts moving through rock and shifting it. Another sign of activity on the mountain was a bulge that formed on one side. **Volcanologists**, scientists who study volcanoes, believed that the bulge was caused by magma flowing up into the mountain. They knew the volcano was getting ready to erupt—but they had no idea when it would happen.

At 8:39 in the morning on May 18, Mount St. Helens erupted with an explosion that blew away a huge chunk of the mountain itself. The shock of the

Mudflows

Mudflows are very dangerous and destructive events caused by violent volcanic eruptions. The heat of the eruption melts snow and ice on the top of the volcano. The water rushes down the mountain, mixing with loose rock and sediments. This mixture becomes thick, like cement, and buries everything in its path.

During the eruption of Mount St. Helens, the mudflows raced down the mountain at 90 miles per hour (145 km/h). When they hit level ground, they slowed down to about 30 miles per hour (48 km/h). At their peak, the mudflows were 44 to 66 feet (13 to 20 m) deep. After most of the liquid drained away, the mudflows covered the ground with mud about 3 feet (0.9 m) thick. Thousands of animals, including deer, bear, and elk, were killed by the mudslides.

When the Nevado del Ruiz volcano in Colombia erupted in November 1985, it melted the snow on the high peak. The mudslide raced down the mountain and poured over the town of Armero, killing 22,000 people.

explosion was felt 200 miles (322 km) away. Within minutes, the hot blast knocked down 150 square miles (390 sq/km) of tall fir trees like tiny matchsticks. A black cloud of gas and ash rose 9 miles (14 km) into the sky. Lightning created in the fast-moving air of the cloud sparked fires that spread over thousands of acres. Melted ice and snow, mixed with red-hot ash and rock, flowed down from the mountain at 90 miles per hour (145 km/hr). The mudflow knocked down steel bridges and houses, and it covered cars. When it flowed into a nearby river, it heated up the water to 100° Fahrenheit (38° Celsius). Fish tried to leap out of the hot water onto land, and millions of salmon died. The hot mudslide made the river flow over its banks and flood the land around it.

Through fires, mudslides, and floods, the eruption of Mount St. Helens killed 57 people that day. Ash blocked out the sunlight and piled up on the ground for hundreds of miles. Carried by the wind in a huge cloud, the ash fell onto almost every state east of the Rocky Mountains.

Volcanoes beneath the Ocean

Not all volcanoes erupt with a sudden explosion. Some flow slowly, like the volcanoes created beneath the oceans. At mid-ocean ridges, hot mantle rises and squeezes out like toothpaste onto the ocean floor. As it cools, it forms new oceanic crust that spreads apart in two directions away from the ridge. Some of the lava can build up into a mountain that reaches above the surface. Iceland is one such mountain. There are still active volcanoes in Iceland, including Askja and Hekla. Eruptions at ocean ridges are weaker than the eruptions of strato-volcanoes, but many more volcanoes are erupting beneath the ocean than are erupting on land.

Hot Spots

The third place that volcanoes can form is over a hot spot. Starting deep within the mantle, maybe even near the core, a *hot spot* is a rising column, or plume, of magma. Hot-spot volcanoes are the largest volcanoes on Earth. After an eruption, more magma begins to seep back up toward the surface to erupt out of the same fissure (crack). For millions of years, a hot spot in the Pacific ocean has been erupting and forming the island of Hawaii. The hot spot stays in the same place, rooted deep within the earth, while the Pacific plate moves in a northwestward direction above it. So the oldest islands in the chain are extinct volcanoes north of the chain. Two of the younger volcanoes are among the biggest in the world,

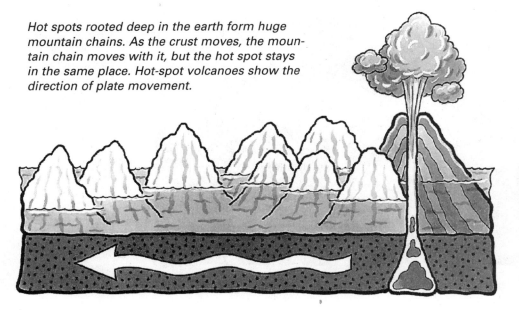

Hot spots rooted deep in the earth form huge mountain chains. As the crust moves, the mountain chain moves with it, but the hot spot stays in the same place. Hot-spot volcanoes show the direction of plate movement.

Mauna Loa and Kilauea. The newest island in the chain, Loihi, has not yet risen above the surface of the water.

Hot-spot eruptions form low slopes called **shield volcanoes.** The lava spreads out from the crater and cools into a gentle slope that looks like a shield.

Types of Eruptions

A volcano is shaped by the type of eruption that brings lava to the surface. There are several ways that magma erupts.

Hawaiian Eruptions

The gentlest volcanic eruptions are a slow and steady release of lava. They are called Hawaiian because the biggest eruptions of this type formed the Hawaiian islands—and continue to form them. Gas does not get trapped with the magma long enough to build up pressure that would cause a big explosion. Kilauea in Hawaii erupts with a string of lava fountains shooting from cracks in the volcano. This amazing curtain of lava can reach 500 feet (152 m) high.

A Hawaiian eruption is calm, with lava flowing to form a gentle slope.

Piton de la Fournaise on Réunion Island in the Indian Ocean is one of the most active volcanoes in the world. It erupts Hawaiian style, spilling runny lava down its slopes about once every 10 months. Piton de la Fournaise means "blazing furnace." The crater at the top of this volcano gives a glimpse of what Earth may have looked like billions of years ago. It is filled with a lake of red-hot magma upon which cooled slabs of rock float and shift around. These crusty slabs are just like the ones that became Earth's continents and plates. By studying the way they move against each other and dip beneath each other, scientists learn more about Earth's tectonic plates.

The Power of Pele

Some Hawaiians believe that Kilauea is the home of Pele, the fire goddess. Every day, dozens of people bring gifts of flowers, rocks, incense, and meat to the volcano to make the goddess happy. Legend says that when Pele is angry, she makes the volcano erupt. Some people have taken rocks from the volcano to take home as souvenirs, only to find that stealing from Pele brings them bad luck. The park rangers at Hawaii Volcanoes National Park get packages in the mail almost every day from people returning stolen rocks, and the rangers put them back on the mountain.

Strombolian Eruptions

The next most powerful type of eruption is named after Stromboli, an island volcano between Italy and Sicily. Stromboli erupts with small explosions about every 15 or 20 minutes, as it has for the past 2,000 years! The explosions are caused by a small buildup of gas in the magma. The lava shoots up about 300 feet (100 m) into the air and falls as ash in and around the crater. The lava is thicker than lava from Hawaiian eruptions. Every few months, the lava flows down a huge crack on the side of the mountain into the sea, *sizzling* and sending up clouds of steam when it hits the water.

Rumbling and hissing when they erupt, Strombolian volcanoes are more noisy than dangerous. They are the most common type of eruption on land. In addition to Stromboli, other Strombolian volcanoes include Parícutin in Mexico and Etna in Sicily.

A Strombolian eruption sends lava a few hundred feet into the air. The weak explosions that sputter from these volcanoes do not create a dangerous lava flow.

Vulcanian Eruptions

The third type of volcanic eruption is named after the volcano that gave volcanoes their name: Vulcano. On the north side of the island of Sicily, Vulcano erupts about once every 100 years. A vulcanian eruption creates much more ash than

Vulcanian eruptions start with a powerful explosion. Small explosions that sound like gunfire can go on for hours, days, months, or years. The danger from vulcanian eruptions comes from huge amounts of ash, not lava.

flowing lava. Eruptions can last for months at a time, as large amounts of ash are blown out by the explosion of volcanic gases. Vulcanian eruptions begin with a violent explosion followed by many loud bangs that sound like gunshots. A vulcanian volcano called Ngauruhoe erupted in New Zealand in February 1975. Every 15 to 50 minutes, eruptions that sounded like gunfire shot from the top of the mountain. After only five hours, it was over, and Ngauruhoe became quiet again. The most active vulcanian performer in our time is the Japanese volcano Sakurajima, which has exploded with small eruptions almost every day since 1955.

Vulcan-ology

The ancient Romans named the mountain Vulcano after the god of fire, Vulcan. They believed the volcano's noisy blasts came from Vulcan's blacksmith workshop, where he hammered red-hot metal into swords on his anvil.

Killer Clouds

Sometimes a cloud filled with hot gas, ash, pumice, and bits of rock is shot out of the volcano like hairspray shot from an aerosol can. This cloud, called a **nuée ardente**, races down the mountain and across the land at speeds up to 300 miles per hour (500 km/h). *Nuée ardente* is a French term that means "heat-glowing cloud." The cloud can be up to 1800° Fahrenheit (1,000° Celsius), and it kills everything it passes. One of the world's worst volcano disasters was a result of a *nuée ardente* that erupted from Mt. Pelée in Martinique (in the Caribbean) in 1902. In the first seconds of this vulcanian eruption, a hot blast shot through the town and instantly killed all 30,000 people.

Plinian Eruptions

The biggest eruptions of them all are named after a man who watched one in A.D. 79. Pliny the Elder witnessed the huge eruption of Mount Vesuvius, which destroyed the nearby cities of Pompeii and Herculaneum. In all the excitement, Pliny died, and his nephew, Pliny the Younger, wrote down his uncle's observations. These writings are the first eyewitness account of a volcanic eruption.

Plinian eruptions, sometimes called vesuvian eruptions, blast out tons of material in an explosion that is the most powerful force on the planet. The explosion can tear chunks of the mountain apart. Ash and pumice shoot through the air at supersonic speeds (faster than sound waves) and rain down to form deep piles on the ground. The hot, gas-filled cloud

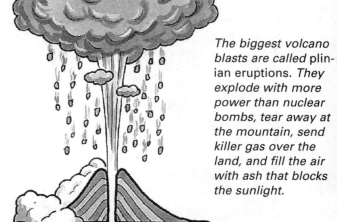

The biggest volcano blasts are called plinian eruptions. *They explode with more power than nuclear bombs, tear away at the mountain, send killer gas over the land, and fill the air with ash that blocks the sunlight.*

towering above the volcano **ignites** lightning and thunderstorms. Ash clings to raindrops and drives down to Earth in hard pellets. More hot, killer gas erupts as *nuées ardentes*. Ash in the atmosphere adds to the terror by blocking the sunlight and putting the entire area in darkness. So much ash is released in plinian eruptions that it is carried by the wind across the entire planet. As the ash forms a layer around Earth, it keeps some of the sun's energy out for months, bringing cooler weather everywhere.

Plinian eruptions are the least common type of volcanic eruptions. They usually have the shortest outburst but cause the greatest amount of destruction. Some of the more recent plinian eruptions include Krakatoa, a volcano on an island in Indonesia, in 1883; Mount St. Helens in Washington in 1980; and Pinatubo in the Philippines in 1991. Plinian eruptions that send out ash covering hundreds of square miles (hundreds of square kilometers) are classified as ultraplinian.

How Big Are Volcanic Eruptions?

The **Volcanic Explosivity Index,** or **VEI,** describes the size of volcanoes based on three observations. A volcano is rated VEI 2, VEI 3, and so forth, based on the violence of the eruption, the height of the plume that shoots out of the vent, and the volume (amount) of material ejected.

VEI Number	Violence of Eruption	Plume Height	Volume	Classification	Total Historic Eruptions
0	Nonexplosive	Less than 100 meters (328 feet)	10^4 m³ (67 cubic miles)	Hawaiian	487
1	Gentle	100–1000 meters (328-3,280 feet)	10^4 m³ (67 cubic miles)	Hawaiian/Strombolian	623
2	Explosive	1–5 km (0.6–3 miles)	10^6 m³ (6,689 cubic miles)	Strombolian/Vulcanian	3,176
3	Severe	3–15 km (1.9–9 miles)	10^7 m³ (66,890 cubic miles)	Vulcanian	733
4	Cataclysmic	10–25 km (6–15.5 miles)	10^8 m³ (668,900 cubic miles)	Vulcanian/Plinian	119
5	Paroxysmal	More than 25 km (more than 15.5 miles)	10^9 m³ (6,689,000 cubic miles)	Plinian	19
6	Colossal	More than 25 km (more than 15.5 miles)	10^{10} m³ (66,890,000 cubic miles)	Plinian/Ultraplinian	5
7		More than 25 km (more than 15.5 miles)	10^{11} m³ (668,900,000 cubic miles)	Ultraplinian	2
8		More than 25 km (more than 15.5 miles)	10^{12} m³ (6,689,000,000 cubic miles)	Ultraplinian	0

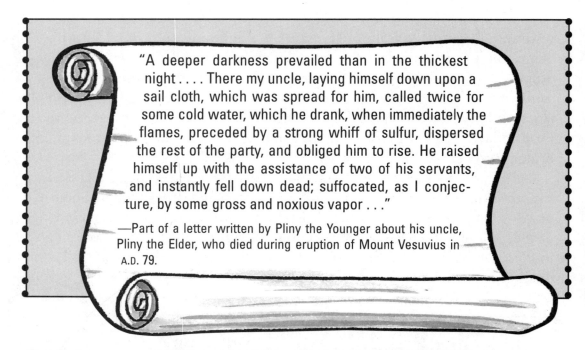

"A deeper darkness prevailed than in the thickest
night . . . . There my uncle, laying himself down upon a
sail cloth, which was spread for him, called twice for
some cold water, which he drank, when immediately the
flames, preceded by a strong whiff of sulfur, dispersed
the rest of the party, and obliged him to rise. He raised
himself up with the assistance of two of his servants,
and instantly fell down dead; suffocated, as I conjec-
ture, by some gross and noxious vapor . . ."

—Part of a letter written by Pliny the Younger about his uncle,
Pliny the Elder, who died during eruption of Mount Vesuvius in
A.D. 79.

Caldera: When Mountains Collapse

After an eruption, the magma chamber becomes hollow. It may not be able to
support the weight of the slopes that surround it. If the slopes cave in, they fill in
the 𝕞𝕒𝕘𝕞𝕒 𝕔𝕙𝕒𝕞𝕓𝕖𝕣 and leave a huge circular opening on the top
of the volcano. This opening can be many miles in diameter and is called a

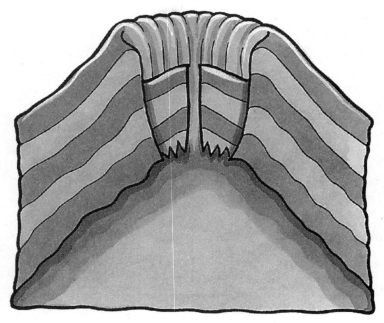

*A hollow magma cham-
ber causes the slopes of
the volcano to collapse.
This creates a wide, deep
opening in the top of the
mountain, called a
caldera.*

caldera. Rain eventually fills the caldera, creating a lake on a mountaintop. The top of the feeder pipe that brings magma to the surface rises from the water in the shape of a cone. A 6-mile-wide, sparkling blue lake fills Crater Lake caldera in Oregon. The caldera was formed after a violent plinian eruption 6,845 years ago. It is 2,000 feet (610 m) deep—the deepest lake in the United States.

Lava Living

Near Dubois, Idaho, a huge, thick lava tube has been turned into a bomb shelter. The entire population of the town, about 2,500 people, can fit into the tube, along with their cars! The tube is stocked with food and water and an electric generator to provide energy.

What Comes out of a Volcano?

Material of all shapes and sizes erupts from volcanoes, from fine ash to chunks of rock than can weigh many tons. Each particle is named for its size.

Size	Name
0.1 inch or less (2 mm)	ash
0.1 to 2.5 inches (2 to 64 mm)	lapilli ("little stones")
2.5 inches and larger (64 mm+)	blocks, when ejected solid; bombs, when ejected soft.

Blocks of solid rock shot into the air can fall miles away from the volcano, can harm or kill people and animals, and can damage buildings, cars, and other objects. *Bombs* are molded into different rounded shapes as they fly through the air. Shooting from the volcano at speeds of about 1,250 miles per hour (2,011 km/h), they can travel about 3 miles (5 km) before landing on the ground. Large bombs may still have melted rock inside. When they hit the ground, they explode and gush red-hot liquid.

Two types of lava flow out of volcanoes. They are given names in the Hawaiian language: *aa* and *pahoehoe*. **Aa** (pronounced "ah-ah") is sharp and twisted, and it cools into a surface that is hard to walk on. (That may be how it got its name—walking over the sharp lava, one might say, "Ah! Ah!") **Pahoehoe** (pronounced "pa-hoy-hoy") is smooth and dries into a shape that looks like rope or twine. Because lava flows slowly, only a few miles per hour, it doesn't pose much of a threat to people. Once a flow has been spotted coming down the mountain, there's time to get out of the way.

Some pahoehoe lava flows form tubes running along the ground. The outer part of the lava cools and forms a hard skin. The liquid lava runs through it, like water through a garden hose. When the lava is drained out, the hollow tube remains. Lava tubes can range from just a few inches (a few centimeters) in diameter to the size of highway or railway tunnels. Many lava tubes are tall and wide enough for people to walk through, like the ones in Victoria, Australia, and at the Kilauea volcano in Hawaii.

Pahoehoe lava flowing from volcanoes beneath the sea forms a skin when it is cooled by the water. As it OOZES out of the vent, it looks like a growing sack, or pillow. When the pillow bursts, lava flows from the tear, and the process begins again. Layers of sea lava look like a pile of pillows and are called **pillow lava.**

Fissure Eruptions: Lava over the Land

Molten rock that erupts from a volcano is a dramatic sight. But magma also comes to the surface in less violent ways. Magma can seep through cracks several miles long and pour over the land. A deep crack in the earth is called a *fissure*, and this type of eruption is called a **fissure eruption.** As the sheet cools, it hardens into a layer of dark gray rock called *basalt*. Another eruption of lava oozing from the crack creates a new layer of basalt rock. Over millions of years, the layers of basalt form a vast, flat plain. In the Pacific

EXPERIMENT

CHOCOLATE LAVA LESSON

With the help of an adult, you can cook up some fudge that shows the difference between aa and pahoehoe lava.

What You Need:
Chocolate fudge mix, and any ingredients required (listed on the box)

Saucepan

2 baking dishes

What to Do:

1. Ask an adult to help you in the kitchen and at the stove. Prepare the fudge mix as directed on the package.
2. When the fudge has begun to boil, pour half of it into a baking dish.
3. Stir the remaining fudge in the saucepan for ten minutes as it cools.
4. Pour the cooled fudge from the saucepan into the second baking dish.
5. Offer your adult helper a piece of fudge.

What Happens and Why:
The fudge that was poured out immediately flows smoothly in the pan, and forms a flat surface. This is like pahoehoe lava. But the fudge that was stirred up as it cooled forms hard little chunks and creates a chunky surface in the baking pan. This is like aa lava.

Northwest of the United States, fissure eruptions have created the Columbia River Plateau and the nearby Snake River Plain.

Layers of basalt rock erupting through **fissures** have also created the Deccan Plateau in India and the Paraná region in South America. Fissure eruptions have flooded places in Mongolia, Siberia, Africa, and Australia. Today, the only place where fissure eruptions occur is in Iceland. Formed by volcanic eruptions on the Mid-Atlantic ridge, Iceland's history is full of lava flows. Volcanic activity, including fissure eruptions, have occurred in Iceland every 5 years for the past 900 years. One third of all the lava that has come to the surface of Earth is found on Iceland.

Lava Plain

Together, the Columbia River Plateau and the Snake River Plain cover 200,000 square miles (518,000 km²). With each eruption, the basalt formed a layer from 40 to 100 feet (9–30 meters) thick. After millions of years of eruptions, the plain is now 3,000 feet (914 meters) thick. The fissures that created these lava areas have been completely covered over and cannot be found.

Can Eruptions Be Predicted?

The biggest clues that a dormant volcano may be coming back to life are earthquakes. Tremors near and beneath the volcano may be caused by magma rising toward the surface and moving the rock around. Volcanologists suspect that a volcano will erupt after earthquakes rumble in the mountain, but they cannot predict when it will happen. A volcano may erupt hours, days, months, or even years after a series of tremors. Seismographs are used to track earthquakes around volcanoes. Volcanologists also measure both the temperature of the volcano and the amount of gases that may be seeping from it. These are clues that something is happening inside. Another clue that magma is rising dangerously close to the surface is the appearance of a bulge on the volcano. This was an important sign that helped volcanologists warn people about Mount St. Helens several weeks before the volcano erupted in 1980. An instrument called a **tiltmeter** records changes in the shape of a volcano and in the land around it. The tiltmeter tells volcanologists when the rock is beginning to bulge by reading changes in the tilt, or angle, of the volcano surface. One type of tiltmeter consists of one or more pots filled with water or **mercury**, with markings on the side to show inches and millimeters. The angle of the liquid in each pot is measured when the tiltmeter is first placed on the surface of the volcano. Then a volcanologist checks the tiltmeter from time to time, measuring the slope of the angle. When the slope changes, it means that the surface of the volcano is changing.

Trapped Magma

Much of the hot rock rising up from the mantle never reaches the surface at all. It cools very slowly and hardens beneath the ground. Magma hardens into igneous rock, and the place where it gathers within the crust is called an **igneous intrusion**. A **batholith** is a large mass of igneous rock formed within the crust. Magma that seeps up through layers of rock and hardens into a wall is called a **dike.** When magma seeps into cracks that spread in horizontal layers, it forms a sheet called a **sill.** Some magma rises near the surface and pushes up on the ground above, forming a dome. The igneous rock that creates the dome is called a **laccolith.**

TILT!

To see how a tiltmeter works, you can build a model one with a few simple objects.

What You Need:
- Two 6-ounce plastic cups

- Pencil

- Modeling clay

- Cookie sheet

- Water

What to Do:
1. Punch a hole in the side of each cup with the sharp end of the pencil.
2. Push one end of the pencil about $\frac{1}{4}$ inch (0.8 mm) into the hole in each cup, forming a rod that connects the cups.
3. With the clay, seal the pencil to the outside of each cup.
4. Fill each cup about half full of water.
5. Place the cups on the cookie sheet.
6. Gently raise one corner of the cookie sheet about 2 inches (51 mm). Notice the angle of the water in the cup nearest you.

What Happens and Why:
The cookie sheet represents the surface of the volcano. The cup closest to you represents the part of the tiltmeter that faces the top of the volcano. When the surface is raised, the water in the cup moves and creates an angle in the cup. This is like the liquid in a tiltmeter. When the surface of the volcano bulges, it moves the tiltmeter, and scientists can measure the amount of change in the surface.

The scientists who study the volcano Merapi in Indonesia, which erupts about every five years, are using the latest in volcanology technology to find changes in the volcano's shape. A mirror is placed high on the mountain, facing down into the valley about 5 miles (8 km) below. Scientists shoot laser beams, or beams of intense light, up at the mirror. The light bounces off the mirror and is sent back to hit a device that measures the distance the beam has traveled. The next time the *laser* is shot, the distance is measured again. If the distance has changed, they know that the mirror has been moved, caused by movement on the mountain. The volcanologists put the measurements into a mathematical formula that will help them learn when the rock is going to break apart. They then try to predict when the rock will give way and cause an eruption.

Volcanoes on Other Planets

Earth is not the only place in the solar system with a history of volcanoes. The atmospheres of all four inner planets—Mercury, Venus, Earth, and Mars—were created by gases blasting to the surface by volcanic activity. Scientists believe that some craters found on several planets and moons were created by volcanoes (though most craters, such as the ones on our moon, were

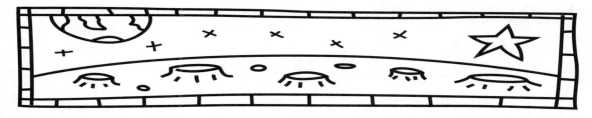

caused by meteorites crashing into the surface). In some regions of Mercury, smooth plains were formed by ancient lava flows. Our moon, Venus, and Mars each have a solid layer of skin shaped by volcanic activity.

The volcanoes on Mercury, Earth's moon, and Mars have been extinct for millions of years. But there are two places in the solar system, other than Earth, where active volcanoes are found.

Venus

In 1992, the spacecraft *Magellan* began sending radar images of Venus back to Earth. Until then, scientists thought that volcanoes had not been active on Venus for hundreds of millions of years. But *Magellan* showed that Venus is dotted with a few active hot spots where lava flows to the surface. There are many different types of volcanic mountains covering Venus, including large, smooth shield volcanoes like the ones found on the Hawaiian Islands. About 800 million years ago, huge lava flows poured over the surface of Venus and cooled into the smooth, rolling plains that cover most of the planet's surface today.

Io, the "Pizza Moon"

One of Jupiter's nine moons, Io (pronounced "eye-oh") is about the same size as Earth's moon. When two *Voyager* spacecraft flew past Io in 1979, each sent back pictures to Earth of a colorful world. The surface of Io is covered with sulfur, a mineral that turns brilliant red, yellow, orange, and brown as it cools and hardens. With these bright colors, Io earned the name of the pizza moon. The Voyagers spotted eight volcanoes erupting at that time, and found about 200 huge calderas. Some of the calderas were filled with red-orange lava lakes. Astronomers looking at Io through a telescope in Mauna Kea, Hawaii, saw a massive eruption in March 1995. They watched a bright spot grow bigger and bigger as the lava spread out over the surface.

In 1996, NASA's *Galileo* spacecraft flew near Io and took more pictures of the moon. Taller volcanoes and new lava flows show that many volcanic eruptions have occurred since the *Voyager* spacecraft flew by 17 years earlier. Things are really cooking on Io!

Olympus Mons

The largest volcano in the solar system is on Mars! Olympus Mons is an extinct volcano that spreads 370 miles (600 km) in diameter. The tallest mountain on Mars, it rises 15 miles (25 km) above a rocky plain. This volcano is almost five times larger than the biggest volcano on Earth, Mauna Loa, which measures 75 miles (120 km) across and is 6 miles (9 km) high.

Mars

Mars is only about half the size of Earth, but its volcanoes are much bigger. The surface of Mars never formed moving plates like those of Earth. So when a hot spot created a volcano at a vent in Mars's surface, the vent stayed in one place. On Earth, the crust would slowly move, and a new volcano would form over the hot spot. On Mars, however, each vent kept pouring out lava for millions of years, creating a huge volcano at each spot.

Volcanoes haven't erupted on Mars for millions of years, but the ancient history of this planet is hot news on Earth these days. In August 1996, NASA announced that living microbes may have existed on Mars more than 3 billion years ago. The clues were found in a 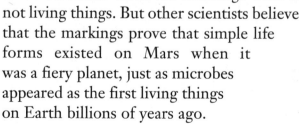 meteorite that landed on Earth about 13,000 years ago. The meteorite came from Mars after another meteorite collided with the planet, sending rock and dust into space. Scientists studied markings in the meteorite that looked like fossils of tiny, one-celled organisms. Some scientists think the markings were made by chemicals, not living things. But other scientists believe that the markings prove that simple life forms existed on Mars when it was a fiery planet, just as microbes appeared as the first living things on Earth billions of years ago.

6

World of Wonders

Killer Quakes and Exploding Mountains

HISTORY-MAKING EARTHQUAKES AND VOLCANOES

For thousands of years, people have lived in areas where earthquakes **rumble** and volcanoes roar. Here are the stories of a few of the most devastating and famous quakes and volcanoes in history.

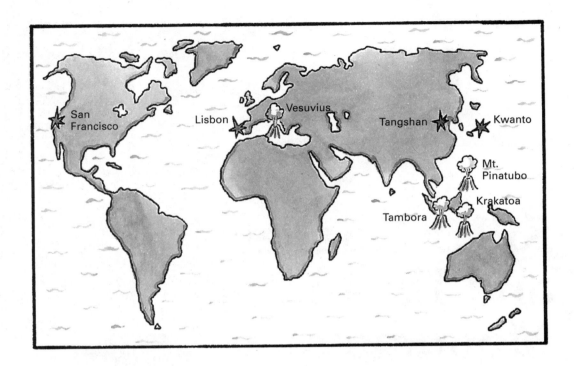

Earthquakes

Lisbon, Portugal, 1755

On November 1, 1755, the narrow streets of Lisbon were filled with people on their way to church. Stone houses and buildings along the curvy little streets blocked the sun, giving shade to the crowds. Lisbon was home to 235,000 people at the time, making it a city about the size of St. Petersburg, Florida, or Rochester, New York, today. Suddenly three great shocks shook the ground and made the surface roll like waves of the sea. The houses tumbled down into the streets, crushing the people below. Candles and oil lamps were knocked over as the buildings shook and fell, igniting fires that spread throughout the city. Those who weren't killed from falling buildings or fires still had to face a giant tsunami rolling in from the ocean. The great quake created a tsunami near the shore that crashed over the city, killing thousands.

By studying the record of the quake, scientists estimate it had a magnitude of 8.7 on the Richter scale. It shook up 1.5 million square miles (4 million km²) of ground and created waves in ponds as far away as England, France, Italy,

Holland, and Switzerland. The quake killed 70,000 people, almost one third of Lisbon's population.

An Englishman named Thomas Chase was living in Lisbon in 1755, and he survived the quake even though his house collapsed. He wrote about his experience many years later in a British magazine. When the ground began to shake, Chase climbed to the top floor of his house to get a better view of what was going on. The house fell down, knocking Chase out and throwing him down into a mountain of rubble. When he woke up, he climbed out of the mess and looked so bloody and horrible that a man passing by jumped back in fright, shouting, "Who are you? Where do you come from?" Chase described his terrible wounds:

My right arm hung down before me motionless, like a great dead weight, the shoulder being out and the bone broken . . . the right ankle swelled to a prodigious size, with a fountain of blood spurting upwards from it . . . all the left side of my face was swelled, the skin beaten off, the blood streaming from it.

San Francisco, 1906

One of the most famous disasters in U.S. history is the earthquake that shook San Francisco on April 18, 1906. At just past five in the morning, police sergeant Jesse Cook was walking his beat on Market Street when he heard a low rumbling sound. Looking down Washington Street, he saw the brick surface moving up and down in waves coming toward him. The great shock came from the San Andreas Fault, 8 miles (13 km) away from the center of the city. The earth rolled with waves 2 feet (0.6 m) high, making buildings weave and fall apart, twisting trolley tracks and streetcars into odd shapes, and creating cracks in the streets that spurted out gas and water from broken pipes. Telegraph and telephone wires were broken, leaving the city cut off from the rest of the world.

Within two hours, 20 huge fires had broken out all over the city. Firefighters could not battle the fires because the earthquake had broken the pipe that brought water from the reservoir south of San Francisco into the city. But near the San Francisco Bay, the Ferry Building was saved by firefighters pumping water from the bay through their fire hoses. Thousands of people made their

The violent shaking during the San Francisco earthquake broke up streets and bent streetcar rails.

way to the Ferry Building, where they could board ferryboats that took them out of the city to safety in Oakland. But elsewhere, San Francisco was in flames. By noon, the entire square mile (2.6 km²) of the city center was burning. That night, the fire brightened the sky 50 miles (81 km) away, so that in the towns of Sonoma and Santa Clara it was light enough outside to read a newspaper.

Sailors from a passing ship came ashore to help repair water pipes and set up new ones from the bay. But the fire grew and created its own wind as the hot air shot up into the sky. The air became so hot that everything near the fire burned or melted. Not until Saturday morning, 74 hours after it began, was the great fire

The City That Wouldn't Die

San Francisco was quickly rebuilt after the great quake and fire of 1906. In October 1909, the city held the Portola Festival to celebrate its recovery.

By that time, many new buildings had been built, and the city was once again an important center for shipping and business.

over. The quake and fire had destroyed 28,000 buildings and 5 square miles (13 km²) of the city. At least 315 people died, and more than 350 others were listed as missing and thought to be dead. The quake was later estimated to be 8.3 on the Richter scale.

The Most Destructive Earthquakes in the World

This chart lists all the earthquakes on record that have caused the deaths of 50,000 or more people, beginning with the highest number of deaths.

Date	Location	Deaths	Magnitude (when available)
January 23, 1556	Shansi, China	830,000	
October 11, 1737	Calcutta, India	300,000	
July 27, 1976	Tangshan, China	255,000	8.0
August 9, 1138	Aleppo, Syria	230,000	
May 22, 1927	Xining, China	200,000	8.3
December 22, 856	Damghan, Iran	200,000	
December 16, 1920	Gansu, China	200,000	8.6
March 23, 893	Ardabil, Iran	150,000	
September 1, 1923	Kwanto, Japan	143,000	8.3
September, 1290	Chihli, China	100,000	
December 28, 1908	Messina, Italy	70,000–100,000	7.5
November, 1667	Shemakha, Caucasia	80,000	
November 18, 1727	Tabriz, Iran	77,000	
November 1, 1755	Lisbon, Portugal	70,000	8.7
December 25, 1932	Gansu, China	70,000	7.6
May 31, 1970	Peru	66,000	7.8
1268	Silicia, Asia Minor	60,000	
January 11, 1693	Sicily, Italy	60,000	
May 30, 1935	Quetta, Pakistan	30,000–60,000	7.5
February 4, 1783	Calabria, Italy	50,000	
June 20, 1990	Iran	50,000	7.7

Kwanto, Japan, 1923

H uge fires were also killers in one of Japan's most deadly earthquakes. In the cities of Yokohama and Tokyo, just before noon on September 1, 1923, many people were home preparing lunch. An 8.2-magnitude quake struck the island, shaking buildings and throwing hot cooking stoves to the floors, where they set furniture, curtains, and other objects on fire. Soon hundreds of buildings were blazing, and a firestorm turned both cities into furnaces. The fire burned everything in sight for two days and finally died out when there was nothing else left to destroy. With its epicenter at the town of Kwanto, the quake killed 143,000 people.

Petroff Skitaretz, a Russian writer who was walking on a hill near Yokohama when the earthquake struck, heard terrifying noises before the ground started shaking:

I thought I heard the sound of an approaching train. I was surprised, for I knew no train ran near there. From somewhere I heard the roaring as of a wild animal. . . . The sound like an underground train came now from directly under our feet, seemingly some pent up, awful energy seeking escape. The angry roaring increased . . . the ground began to move, groaning and yanking us back and forth . . . we felt as though we were about to be torn to pieces.

September 1 is "disaster day" in Tokyo, in memory of the great Kwanto earthquake. Every year on this day, people practice safety drills, such as target practice with buckets of water, that will help them survive the next earthquake.

Tangshan, China, 1976

In the early morning hours of July 28, 1976, the ground started to shake beneath the city of Tangshan. With its focus nearly 7 miles (11 km) directly beneath the city, the great Tangshan earthquake sent out shock waves 400 times greater than an atomic bomb. About 255,000 people were crushed to death when most of the buildings collapsed into heaps of rubble. Many of those who survived in the city and the surrounding area were among the 600,000 seriously hurt.

The huge number of deaths from the Tangshan earthquake made it a tragedy that caught the world's attention. But the amazing survival rate of a nearby county also caught the attention of earthquake safety experts around the world. This

8.0-magnitude quake destroyed more than 180,000 buildings in Qinglong County, 71 miles (115 km) from Tangshan—but only one person died. County officials had taken action several days before the earthquake hit, gathering information from hundreds of stations set up to look for earthquake warning signs. In one high school, for example, a student team assigned to observe animal behavior reported that weasels and rats were moving around in broad daylight, unafraid of humans. Another **warning sign** was reported on July 24, when people noticed that natural springwater had become muddy. This showed that forces were at work below the surface, moving mud and rock into underground water supplies.

Based on these observations, county officials set up tents and evacuated 60 percent of the population—470,000 people. Those who did not move out of their homes were instructed to keep their doors and windows open at all times, to avoid being trapped when the earthquake hit. The only victim of the earthquake in Qinglong County was a man who died from a heart attack. Hundreds of thousands of people were saved by paying attention to nature's earthquake warning signs. The United Nations has studied Qinglong County's system, which brings together information from scientists and the public. The mix of science and community involvement added up to saved lives in China, and the United Nations is sharing Qinglong's story with the world.

Volcanoes

Two violent and deadly eruptions, Mount St. Helens in 1980 and Mount Pelée in 1902, illustrated the awesome power of different types of eruptions in chapter 5. Here are the stories of four other volcanoes that have blasted their way into the world's record books.

The Discovery of Pompeii

The first official **excavation** (the uncovering of a buried site) of Pompeii began in 1860, when the king of Italy appointed Giuseppe Fiorelli to head the project. Fiorelli invented a method for creating sculpture of the bodies found in Pompeii. Over time, the ash became solid rock and the bodies trapped inside decayed. The outlines of the bodies were left behind as hollows in the rock. Bones also remained inside the hollows. When Fiorelli discovered the outline of a body, he filled the cavity with wet plaster of Paris. The plaster dried into the shape of the body, showing the terrified poses of people trying to breathe and huddling together for protection.

Vesuvius, A.D. 79

With an eruption nearly 2,000 years ago that hasn't been matched in Europe to this day, Vesuvius is the world's most famous volcano. In the year A.D. 79, after being dormant for hundreds of years, the volcano came to life with one of the most violent eruptions in history. The blast was totally unexpected and killed nearly 3,400 people in the nearby towns of Pompeii and Herculaneum.

Four days before the eruption, several earthquakes shook the ground around Vesuvius. The 20,000 people living in Pompeii, 6.2 miles (10 km) southeast of the mountain, did not imagine that the volcano was about to erupt. Vesuvius was a gentle, sloping mountain covered with rich soil and vineyards that supplied grapes for wine. At one o'clock in the afternoon on August 24, the top of the mountain exploded. The blast sent a column of gas and ash

20 miles (32 km) into the air, creating a dark cloud that could be seen for many miles. In Misenum, 18 miles (30 km) away across the bay, the cloud caught the attention of Pliny the Elder, his wife, and his nephew (Pliny the Younger). Pliny the Younger's description of the volcano is the first written account of a volcanic eruption.

For the next seven hours, winds carried the ash to Pompeii, covering the city in about 4.6 feet (1.4 m) of white ash and pumice. Roofs collapsed under the weight as panicked crowds fled the city. After midnight, the eruption changed from an outflow of ash to a hot, deadly *nuée ardente*. The first killer cloud raced down the mountain and reached Herculaneum in less than 4 minutes. The hot, swirling cloud covered the town, killing hundreds of people as they choked on the poisonous gas. Two more *nuées ardentes* blasted from the volcano, finishing off any survivors in Herculaneum while gray pumice continued to fall on Pompeii.

At 7:30 in the morning on August 25, another violent *nuée ardente* blasted from Vesuvius, this time headed for Pompeii. The hot, speeding cloud blew off the tops of buildings and killed the remaining 2,000 people in the town. Some were crushed by falling columns or bricks, some were baked by the heat, others were

Was Atlantis Destroyed by a Volcano?

In the fourth century B.C., Plato wrote about an island called Atlantis that disappeared beneath the sea. The legend of Atlantis has been a mystery ever since. No one knows whether it really existed or, if it did, what great disaster caused it to sink into the ocean. Scientists have a theory that Atlantis was once an island in the Aegean Sea south of Greece. Volcanologists have learned that around 1500 B.C., the Strogili volcano erupted with such a force that the entire island blew apart and disappeared. More eruptions beneath the sea built up the island again, which is now called Thira, and sometimes called Santorini. It's possible that Atlantis was the civilization on Strogili, lost forever in one huge, fiery blast.

The Volcano That Created Frankenstein

During the "cold summer" of 1816, caused by the eruption of Mount Tambora, writer Mary Wollstonecraft was on vacation in Switzerland. To pass the time during the cold, rainy weather, Mary and her friends, the poet Percy Bysshe Shelley (whom she would soon marry) and Lord Byron, wrote ghost stories. Next to the warm glow of the fireplace, they read their stories aloud to amuse and entertain each other. Mary's story turned out to be much more than a rainy day tale. In 1818, it was published and became Mary Shelly's most famous book, *Frankenstein*.

poisoned by the gases, and many were choked by the hot ash that filled their lungs with every breath.

When the great eruption ended on the morning of August 26, Herculaneum was buried under 75 feet (23 m) of ash. Pompeii was lost beneath 10 feet (3 m) of ash. The two towns were forgotten for hundreds of years. But when Vesuvius erupted again in 1631, killing nearly 4,000 people, the ancient cities were discovered. As workers began rebuilding, they **uncovered** sections of the ancient city of Pompeii.

Pompeii opens a window into daily life in Italy 2,000 years ago. Round loaves of bread were found in ovens, bowls of figs and walnuts sat on tabletops waiting to be eaten. Beautiful color pictures made of tiles decorated the floors and walls, and jewelry from that era reveals the skill of ancient artists.

Vesuvius is a dangerous and deadly volcano that has erupted more than 30 times since A.D. 79. The most recent eruption was in 1944, when huge amounts of ash were blown into the air and lava flowed in a smoky path through nearby towns.

Tambora, Indonesia, 1815

In the spring of 1815, the volcano Mount Tambora began an eruption bigger than the world had seen in 10,000 years. Tambora is on the island Sumbawa, east of Bali in the Java Sea. After several days of eruptions, the volcano had blown off 4,200 feet (1.3 km) from the top of the mountain. Tons of ash were sent into the atmosphere, bringing darkness for three days to an area covering 200 miles (322 km). Volcanic ash and pumice formed a 1-foot-thick layer on the surface of the sea. Four years later, sailors still found big chunks of pumice floating in the water. Only 26 of the 12,000 people living on the island survived the volcano. The ash that fell on nearby islands covered up soil and crops and caused the deaths of 82,000 more people from starvation.

Meanwhile, the ash floating high in the atmosphere was taken by winds throughout the world. It caused a haze that made the sun appear dull and reddish in the sky. Tambora filled the sky with so much ash that it turned the seasons upside-down on the other side of the planet. The following spring, millions of people in North America and Europe experienced the strangest weather they had ever known. In June 1816, the eastern part of the United States was hit with snow and frost. Farmers had just planted their crops, but the frost killed the seeds beneath the ground. Suddenly the cold snap ended, temperatures rose, and farmers planted again. But in early July, the cold returned again and froze the ground. In Canada, lakes were frozen over in the middle of the summer. Late in August, snowstorms and frost shut down the farming season for good.

In Europe, the "cold summer" of 1816 was very destructive. Cold weather and heavy rains ruined the summer harvest, and thousands of people died of starvation. Weakened from hunger, people came down with a disease called *typhus*, which spread quickly throughout Europe and killed about 200,000 people. All over the world, 1816 was known as "The Year without a Summer."

Krakatoa, Indonesia, 1883

Like Tambora, Krakatoa is an island volcano in the Java Sea. After 200 years of quiet, Krakatoa burst into action on May 20, 1883. The eruption spilled ash 522 miles (840 km) north in Singapore, 718 miles (1,155 km) southwest on Cocos

Island, and on ships as far as 3,776 miles (6,076 km) out to sea. But Krakatoa had just begun to cook. For the next three months, the volcano rumbled and shook. On August 26 and 27, the mountain erupted with explosions that were heard 2,000 miles (3,200 km) away in Australia, and more than 3,000 miles (4,800 km) away in distant Mauritius, an island east of Africa. The explosions caused giant waves to form at sea, which crashed over nearby islands and killed 36,417 people. At least one of the tsunamis rolling in from the ocean was 100 feet (30 m) high, crushing entire villages when it hit land. Twelve hours after one of the explosions, a sea wave from Krakatoa had traveled 3,800 nautical miles (sea miles) to the coast of Yemen on the Arabian Sea.

Krakatoa's great eruption changed the face of the mountain forever. When it was over, only one third of the island was left standing above sea level. The rest had been blasted away from the explosions. The volcano sent 5 cubic miles (20 km³) of ash into the atmosphere, which created deep colors in the evening skies around the world for months.

Krakatoa Offspring

Krakatoa lies in an area of strong volcanic activity, the Pacific Ocean's Ring of Fire. In 1952, a new volcano poked its head above the surface right next to Krakatoa. This small island has been named Anak Krakatoa, which means "Child of Krakatoa."

Pinatubo, Philippines, 1991

Before 1991, Mount Pinatubo was considered so safe that the American Air Force built a base nearby. The volcano had not erupted since the Spaniards settled the Philippines in 1541. But on the afternoon of April 2, 1991, a crack opened near the top of the mountain and erupted with ash that fell on villages 6.2 miles (10 km) away. The next day, the crack grew longer, and 5,000 people were moved away from the most dangerous areas near the volcano.

The Deadliest Volcanic Eruptions in the World

These eruptions have caused the deaths of at least 500 people. Other eruptions have been more powerful, but no one lived close enough to them to be harmed.

Deaths	Volcano	When	Major Cause of Death
92,000	Tambora, Indonesia	1815	Starvation
36,417	Krakatoa, Indonesia	1883	Tsunami
29,025	Mt. Pelée, Martinique	1902	Ash flows
25,000	Ruiz, Columbia	1985	Mudflows
14,300	Unzen, Japan	1792	Volcano collapse, tsunami
9,350	Laki, Iceland	1783	Starvation
5,110	Kelkut, Indonesia	1919	Mudflows
4,011	Galunggung, Indonesia	1882	Mudflows
3,500	Vesuvius, Italy	1631	Mudflows
3,360	Vesuvius, Italy	79	Ash flows and falls
2,942	Lamington, Papua N. GI	1951	Ash flows
2,000	El Chichon, Mexico	1982	Ash flows
1,680	Soufrière, S. Vincent	1902	Ash flows
1,475	Oshima, Japan	1741	Tsunami
1,377	Asama, Japan	1783	Ash flows, mudflows
1,335	Taal, Philippines	1911	Ash flows
1,200	Mayon, Philippines	1814	Mudflows
1,184	Agung, Indonesia	1963	Ash flows
1,000	Cotopaxi, Ecuador	1877	Mudflows
800	Pinatubo, Philippines	1991	Roof collapses and disease
700	Komagatake, Japan	1640	Tsunami
700	Ruiz, Colombia	1845	Mudflows
500	Hibok-Hibok, Philippines	1951	Ash flows

Seismographs were set on Pinatubo, and a volcano observation station was set up at Clark Air Base. In the following weeks, nearly 2,000 small earthquakes were detected near the volcano. In early June, a *bulge* appeared on the mountain, and the volcano team warned that a major eruption could occur any day. By June 9, 25,000 people had been evacuated from the area surrounding the volcano. The next day, 14,000 Americans were also moved out of Clark Air Base.

On June 12, Philippine Independence Day, Pinatubo started the holiday with a bang. Major eruptions sent a column of ash 12 miles (19 km) into the air at a speed of 37 miles per hour (60 km/hour). Thousands more people were evacuated, and just in time. Two days later, the most violent phase of Pinatubo's eruption began. For hours, a giant column of ash and pumice shot up from the volcano, and many *nuées ardentes* blasted down its slopes. As the lava left the volcano, the walls began crashing in and a caldera, 1.2 miles (2 km) in diameter, was formed. Pinatubo was suddenly 984 feet (300 m) shorter.

When it was over, Pinatubo had covered thousands of acres of farmland with thick ash. Most of the people of the Aetna tribe, who had lived on the slopes of the mountain, had lost their traditional homeland. Even though thousands of people had been moved out of danger in time, 300 people died from the eruption. Five hundred more people died of diseases they caught in the crowded centers they were forced to live in during the eruption.

Ash clouds from Pinatubo were carried by winds over the entire earth. Just as the Tambora volcano had done in the early 1800s, this volcano caused colder weather in distant places. Blocking out some of the sun's heat, the ash caused early snowfalls in the autumn of 1992 in Alaska, Scotland, Moscow, and Switzerland. That year, Britain had the coldest October anyone could remember. In the summer and autumn of 1993, stormy weather over North America and Europe brought damaging floods.

World of Wonders

Why Is Old Faithful *Not* So Faithful?

GEYSERS AND OTHER HOT STUFF

The same Earth forces that create volcanoes work their power on underground water, too. Superheated water that makes its way to the surface takes the form of **hot springs** and geysers.

How Does Water Get Underground?

When rain falls on the ground, some of it flows over the surface as **runoff.** Some soaks into the soil and the roots of plants. But some seeps further below the surface into the rocks and becomes **groundwater.**

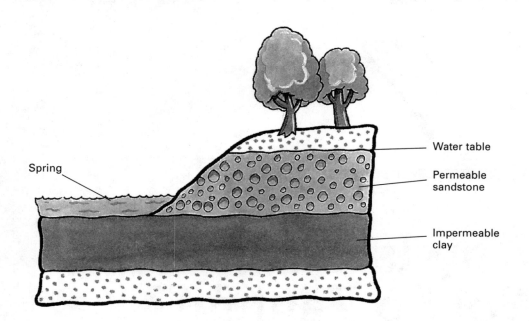

Spring

Water table

Permeable
sandstone

Impermeable
clay

Rocks that can let water flow through them are called **permeable rocks.**
Sandstone is a permeable rock, containing tiny holes that water can pass
through, like a sponge. Other permeable rocks, such as granite
and limestone, contain cracks that allow water to enter. Rocks that water cannot
flow through, such as clay, are called **impermeable rocks.** The top of a layer of
permeable rock is the water table. Wherever the water table reaches to the surface, water flows out as a spring, lake, swamp, or oasis in the desert.

Geysers—Earth's Fancy Plumbing

Underground water that erupts through a vent in the surface is a geyser. There
are three things that must be present to create a geyser:

1. a large water supply
2. intense heat
3. special underground plumbing—in other words, a network of channels
   through a special kind of rock

Geysers are very rare because this combination is not easy to find in nature.
There are only about 600 geysers on Earth, and 400 of them are found in
Yellowstone Park in the United States. Water and heat are easy to find within the
earth, but the right kind of rock is hard to come by. For water to be thrown into
the air, the rock "pipes" must be of a type that keeps the water from seeping out.
The rock that makes the best kind of seal is volcanic rock called **rhyolite.**

The Original Geyser

All the geysers in the world get their name from a geyser in Iceland. *Geysir,* which means "gusher," is a geyser located northwest of Reykjavik, Iceland's capital. Geysir was first described by an English monk in 1294.

His written notes are the first detailed, precise description of a geyser in history. Geysir rarely erupts, but when it does, the eruption may reach 200 feet (61 m).

How Does a Geyser Erupt?

A geyser consists of a rock tube in the ground that goes as deep as 300 feet (92 m) below the surface of the earth. The tube contains many sharp bends and is narrow in some spots and wider in others. Small open spaces called **reservoirs** are connected to the main tube. Groundwater flows into the reservoirs and is heated by the hot rocks that surround it. The water at the bottom of the geyser heats up higher than the boiling point—212° Fahrenheit (100° Celsius)—but it doesn't boil. The pressure of all the water above it prevents the water from boiling.

The lining of the pipes holds the superheated water in, as more water keeps flowing into the reservoirs from the permeable rocks that surround the pipes. As the temperature rises, a few bubbles of steam float up to the surface. When the bubbles rise out of the vent, some of the pressure on the hot water in the geyser is reduced and more steam bubbles form. When these bubbles escape, they lower the pressure even more. When more and larger steam bubbles try to force themselves through the crooked and narrow spaces, they squirt through and push the water on top of them out of the geyser. The reduced pressure allows more of the water to *boil*, sending huge amounts of steam through the pipes. When the geyser erupts, steam and hot water shoot out violently from the vent in the ground.

An eruption ends when the water is used up or when the temperature drops below the boiling point. After the eruption, the cycle of filling, heating, boiling, and erupting begins again. Small geysers can fill again in a few seconds, but bigger ones take hours, days, or even months to fill.

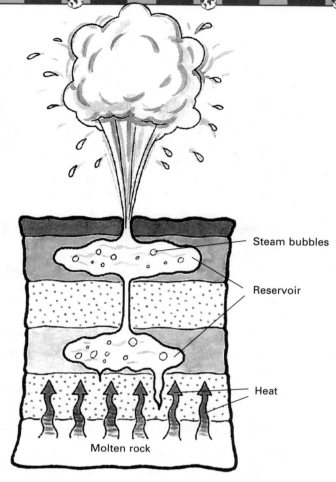

Steam bubbles

Reservoir

Heat

Molten rock

ach geyser is different, and some may erupt before they are completely full. Some may be full for a long time before they are hot enough to erupt, and water will gently flow out of the vent until the eruption occurs. In many geysers, minerals, sand, and clay from inside the earth are mixed with the hot water and steam. After many eruptions, some of these materials build up around the vent to create a round structure called a **cone.**

Do All Geysers Erupt at Regular Intervals?

Water is always flowing into a geyser, but only a few geysers erupt with a regular schedule. These are called **regular geysers** and include Old Faithful in Yellowstone National Park. Most geysers are irregular, with ever-changing time intervals between eruptions. The plumbing system of most geysers is connected to other geysers. Hot water from one system can begin flowing into another geyser, taking the steam out of the first geyser. For example, in Yellowstone, Daisy Geyser was once a very large and regular geyser, while the nearby vent called Bonita Pool only overflowed slightly. When the hot water began to flow into Bonita's pipes in the 1950s, it took energy away from Daisy. For the next 13 years, Daisy only erupted three times, and Bonita flowed heavily and spurted with many small eruptions. Then, in the 1970s, the flow began going back toward Daisy. Today, Daisy is once again a strong and regular geyser, and Bonita is quiet.

One hundred years ago, Old Faithful was described in advertisements as a geyser that erupted "every hour on the hour." But over the years, America's most famous geyser has been slowing down. In 1950, the average interval between eruptions was 62 minutes. In 1970, it had stretched out to 66 minutes, and today

What's That Smell?

When I visited Yellowstone, I had to plug my nose when I got near the hot springs. In addition to water and steam, hot streams flow with sulfur gas, which smells like rotten eggs!

the geyser erupts about every 77 minutes. Twenty years ago, Old Faithful was easier to predict, with eruptions occurring within 5 minutes of the expected time. Now the geyser's eruptions can come 10 minutes sooner or later than the regular 77-minute interval.

Why is Old Faithful becoming less faithful? Scientists believe that mild earthquakes in Yellowstone are shaking the rock that makes up the geyser system. Tremors can break open new cracks that make new pathways for groundwater. Some of the water that has always flowed into Old Faithful has been rerouted to other geysers. With less water and less water pressure, Old Faithful is very slowly losing steam.

Earthquakes aren't the only **shake-ups** that can change the delicate balance of geysers. Hot water beneath the ground has been used for **geothermal energy,** by leading the hot water to machines in a power plant. The steam moves a machine called a *turbine*, which then creates electricity that is used in houses, schools, and other buildings in towns and cities. By taking the hot water away from geyser systems, geothermal energy destroys geyser activity.

Another danger to geysers comes from the people who visit them. For the past 125 years, curious people have thrown all kinds of things into Old Faithful, just to see what happens. Sometimes objects shoot back out, but some also get caught in the geyser and clog up the pipes. In the 1880s, soldiers camped in Yellowstone joked in letters to their families about cleaning their blue uniforms in Old Faithful. According to these tall tales, they threw their blue uniforms into the geyser and the uniforms came back out pressed, folded, and with a laundry tag. But clogging up geysers is no joke. Tourists have thrown pieces of furniture, buckets, tree logs, beer cans, coins, rifle shells, and clothes into Yellowstone's geysers, plugging up some of them for good.

Even though there has been a slight change in Old Faithful's timing, it is still one of the most regular geysers in the world. With each eruption, Old Faithful shoots a column of water at least 100 feet (31 m) into the air. Eruptions have been higher than 180 feet (55 m). The water rockets into the sky for a **duration** of $1\frac{1}{2}$ to 5 minutes, then the geyser becomes quiet as it fills. Within about 77 minutes, it will erupt again—guaranteed!

Hot Springs

Extremely hot water that flows out to the surface is a **hot spring**. These springs are different than geysers because they do not erupt, but flow out over the ground. The water in a hot spring does not get superheated like water in a geyser, because the plumbing of a hot spring allows cool, incoming water to mix with hot water. A geyser is a special type of hot spring and is always found in an area of hot springs called a **geyser basin**.

Where Are Hot Springs and Geysers Found?

The major geyser basins of the world are found in Yellowstone, Iceland, New Zealand, Chile, and Russia's Kamchatka. Other geyser basins throughout the world are found in Turkey, Mexico, Peru, the Azores Islands, Ethiopia, Kenya,

Japan, Tibet, Thailand, Indonesia, and Papua New Guinea. In the United States, hot springs and geysers are also found in California, Nevada, and Alaska.

Yellowstone National Park, Wyoming

Yellowstone contains by far the largest share of the world's geysers, with 9 geyser basins and more than 400 geysers. The other major geyser areas are much smaller, each containing about 25 geysers or fewer. Creating the steamy fields of Yellowstone is a giant magma chamber that lies below eastern Yellowstone park. The geysers of Yellowstone only hint at the mighty forces lying below the surface of Wyoming.

Volcanic activity has erupted from this chamber once about every 600,000 to 800,000 years. The first eruption, 2 million years ago, blasted 15,000 times more ash and lava into the sky than the amount blown out by Mount St. Helens in 1980! Six hundred thousand years ago, another huge eruption blasted from the chamber and created a vast caldera when the chamber collapsed. Most of Yellowstone National Park lies within the caldera, which is 28 miles wide and 47 miles long (45 km by 75 km). Heat rising from the magma chamber heats up the surrounding rocks. Groundwater seeping through the rocks is heated up and enters the plumbing of each geyser basin. Scientists predict that another volcanic eruption could occur from this hot spot beneath Wyoming, but it's impossible to predict exactly when.

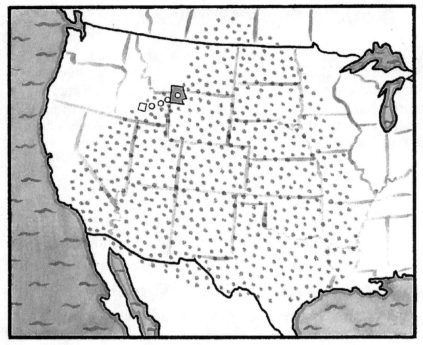

The hot spot beneath Wyoming has caused volcanic eruptions for millions of years. As the North American plate moved over the hot spot, the eruptions left a line of calderas now called Oregon's Craters of the Moon National Monument.

Iceland

Hot springs are a common part of the landscape over much of Iceland. There are 30 geysers on the island, making it one of the most important geyser fields on Earth. The most active geyser basin is in the exact center of the island at a place called Hveravellir. It contains about 15 active geysers, but most of them are small. The largest one erupts to a height of 15 feet (4.6 m).

The geyser with the highest eruptions in Iceland is Strokkur, which erupts about every 15 to 20 minutes. The fountain of water and steam usually jets about 75 feet (23 m) into the air.

Many of the geysers in Iceland have lost the power to erupt because of drilling for geothermal energy. Iceland does not have any other natural energy resources, such as gas, coal, or oil, so geothermal energy is important for heating the country's homes and buildings.

New Zealand

The second largest collection of geyser basins in the world is on North Island of New Zealand in the Pacific Ocean. In the past, about 200 active geysers spouted their stuff throughout the basin. But modern times have brought drilling for geothermal energy and reduced the number of geysers to about 40.

The most active geyser area today is in a park called the Maori Preserve. The geysers inside the park are protected from geothermal drilling, but drilling outside the park has also affected some of the geysers. One active geyser in this basin is Te Horo, which shoots up about 50 feet (15 m) every two hours. Near Te Horo is the Prince of Wales Feathers Geyser, which erupts at the same time. This geyser shoots out at an angle from a mound, creating streams of water and steam that look like giant feathers.

Chile

High in the Andes mountains, surrounded by active volcanoes, lies the third largest geyser basin in the world. El Tatio has formed up to 67 geysers, but they have not all been active at the same time. This basin contains small geysers, with the highest eruptions measuring about 20 feet (6 m). The location of El Tatio, 13,800 feet (4,206 m) above sea level, makes it one of the most distinctive geyser sites on the planet. The geyser basin is heated up by the same molten rock that fuels the surrounding volcanoes.

Kamchatka, Russia

The long piece of land that juts down into the Pacific Ocean on the eastern coast of Russia is called the Kamchatka Peninsula. Along a 2-mile stretch of the Geysernaya River lie 22 geysers. This river valley is called the Valley of Geysers and lies in a remote part of Russia that was not explored until 1941. Discovered

Hot Springs Paint Flamingos Pink

In the volcanic regions of Ethiopia and Kenya, large deposits of ash spread over the land. This ash contains soda, a common white substance used in toothpaste and cleaning products. When rainwater filled the low-lying areas of soda-covered land, they created soda lakes. Hot springs also carry more soda to the lakes from inside the earth. The soda lakes are home to long-necked, pink birds called flamingos. The lakes are also home to algae that the flamingos swallow when they drink the water. The algae contain a chemical that gives the flamingos their pink color. These beautiful birds owe their amazing color to the volcanic activity of the earth!

by a woman scientist named T. I. Ustinova, the valley was recognized as a rare place and soon became Kronotski National Park.

One of the park's geysers is called "The Three" because it shoots out from three vents at different angles. The Three erupts several times every day, jetting up to 75 feet (23 m) each time. Joining The Three in these eruptions is a nearby geyser called "Neighbor," which erupts at the same time. The largest geyser in the basin is Velikan, which means "giant." Every four to six hours, this geyser shoots a fountain of water and steam up more than 130 feet (40 m), making it one of the largest geysers in the world.

Hot Springs' Colors and Shapes

The minerals that flow out of hot springs cover the ground and dry into odd shapes and layers of many colors. In Yellowstone's Mammoth Hot Springs, two tons of minerals spurt out from the earth every day. As the hot water cools and evaporates, the minerals group together to form terraces, columns, and other shapes. Iron colors the surface red, brown, and black; sulfur gives off a yellow hue; and other minerals paint the ground white, shades of gray, and other colors. Early visitors to Yellowstone were amazed by the color and design of the hot-spring basins, and compared them to imaginary fairylands:

. . . *painted in every color of the brightest rainbow, and magically carved . . . one becomes enchanted with this delightful realm, and calls to mind all that he had heard or read about the airy phantoms and . . . water-sprites of mythological tales.*

Soaking Up the Springs

Many people believe that hot springs contain minerals that are good for the body. When thousands of hot springs were discovered in Yellowstone, people with health problems were invited to visit them. Advertisements claimed that the springs would help people who had aching joints, breathing problems, bad blood circulation, and many other health problems. Today, strict rules keep visitors from being burned in the hot springs. The only safe places to enjoy the warmth of the springs are in creeks where hot water joins the cold stream. On a cold winter day, Yellowstone Park workers may reward themselves with a dip in a steaming, gently rolling stream. These natural "hot tubs" take off the winter chill as workers relax their tired muscles.

In Japan, hot springs are very popular places to soak up the warmth that comes from deep within the earth. In the ninth century, Mount Tsurumi erupted and created a field of hot water and rock beneath Beppu on the island of Kyushu. The volcano has been dormant since then, but it created a geyser basin containing 4,000 hot springs. The mineral springs form pools of warm mud called *jigoku*, which are used as mud baths.

Tiny living organisms called *bacteria* and *algae* that live in the geyser basin also give off beautiful colors. The organisms get their energy from the chemicals in the gases that come out of the springs.

Fumaroles, Mud Pots, and Spouters

Geyser basins and other volcanic areas contain more than hot springs and geysers. A **fumarole**, from the Latin word *fumus* which means "smoke," shoots out steam and hot gases instead of water. Often called *steam vents*, fumaroles are found on higher ground than hot springs. Jets of steam hiss and growl as they shoot through the vent. Beneath the ground, boiling water can be heard as it churns.

Some springs flow with clay, mud, and minerals rather than water. These oozing pools are called **mud pots.** Some mud pots are soupy and runny, while others that carry almost no moisture are hard and half-baked from the heat below. Mud pots can be gray, black, white, or cream-colored. Rare mud pots, called **paint pots**, are colored bright red or pink from iron in the mud.

When steam shoots through a mud pot, the outburst creates **fantastic shapes** in the muck, including waves, thick bumps or knobs, fanned-out layers that look like flower petals, and other designs. When the mud pot is runny, it throws up blobs that pile up into a cone or mound called a **mud volcano.** The mud pots in Yellowstone come in many sizes, from small holes in the ground to kettle-shaped heaps 33 feet (10 m) wide and 16 feet (5 m) deep.

Geysers that continuously jet with water and steam, with no quiet periods in between, are called **perpetual spouters.** Papakura Geyser in New Zealand is a typical perpetual spouter, shooting jets of steam and water in several directions 24 hours a day. Yosimoto Geyser in Japan and Imperial Geyser in Yellowstone change from geysers to spouters from time to time. After a period of erupting at regular intervals, changes in the plumbing beneath the surface turn them into perpetual spouters, erupting without a break.

Glossary

aa: lava that forms in jagged blocks and creates a rough surface.

accretion: the step-by-step buildup of large objects such as planets and moons.

aftershock: a tremor that occurs after the largest shock of an earthquake.

archaea: very tiny organisms that live in the hot, poisonous waters near deep ocean vents.

ash: small particles sent into the air during a volcanic eruption.

aurora borealis: ribbons of color in the sky created when particles of energy streaming from the Sun hit Earth's magnetic poles.

batholith: a large mass of igneous rock within Earth's crust.

black smoker: a vent on the ocean floor, which erupts with hot gas that looks like smoke.

body waves: a seismic wave that travels through Earth's interior.

caldera: an area on a volcano formed by the collapse of the volcano walls.

carbonate: a type of rock-forming mineral that forms limestone and dolomite.

compound: a substance made of two or more different kinds of atoms.

condensation: the process by which water vapor becomes liquid water.

cone: the shape of a strato-volcano; narrow at the top and gradually wider toward the base. The cone is formed by layers of lava as they cool.

continental drift: a theory that the continents float over Earth's crust; now replaced by the theory of plate tectonics.

convection current: the pattern of movement of air and water when they are heated.

core: the innermost section of Earth, made of solid iron.

crust: the outer layer of Earth, forming a thin "skin" of rock.

dike: a wall of rock within Earth's crust, formed by rising magma that cools and hardens.

dormant volcano: an inactive volcano that is expected to erupt again in the future.

duration: the period of time in which a geyser is erupting.

element: a material made of a cluster of atoms that cannot be broken down into different kinds of atoms.

epicenter: the point on Earth's surface directly above the focus of an earthquake.

excavation: the scientific uncovering of buried objects.

extinct volcano: a volcano that is not active and is not expected to erupt again.

fault: a region in Earth's crust where rock has broken and slipped.

fault creep: slow movement along a fault, allowing a continuous release of pressure.

feeder pipe: a narrow tunnel leading from a magma chamber to the surface of a volcano.

fissure eruption: an event in which magma seeps through deep cracks in Earth and pours over the surface.

focus: the point within Earth where the first movements of an earthquake begin.

foreshock: an earthquake tremor that occurs before the largest shock.

fossil: the imprint of a living object made in rock.

fumarole: a vent on the surface of Earth that erupts with steam and hot gases.

galaxy: a collection of gas, dust, planets, and billions of stars. Earth is located in the Milky Way galaxy.

geologist: a scientist who studies the physical history and structure of Earth.

geothermal energy: electrical energy created in a turbine, using hot water from beneath the surface of Earth.

geyser basin: an area of land containing hot springs, some of which may be geysers.

Geysir: a geyser in Iceland from which all geysers get their name.

gravity: the force that pulls matter together.

groundwater: rainwater that has seeped below the surface into layers of rock.

guyot: a flat, underwater volcanic mountain that has been eroded by waves.

hot spring: a flow of extremely hot water from beneath the ground out to the surface.

hydrothermal vent: a hot spring on the ocean floor.

igneous rock: rock made from molten material.

igneous intrusion: magma that does not reach the surface but cools and hardens into rock within the crust.

impermeable rock: rock that water cannot flow through, such as clay.

intensity: a description of the physical damage caused by an earthquake.

laccolith: magma that rises near the surface and pushes up on the ground above to form a dome.

land bridge: a series of islands connecting the continents, used in a theory to explain why similar fossils are found in Africa and South America.

lava: magma that has escaped to the surface of Earth.

lithosphere: the upper part of the mantle and the entire crust, containing the tectonic plates of Earth.

Love waves: an earthquake surface wave that moves the surface from side to side.

magma chamber: a pool of magma beneath a volcano.

magnet: an object covered with a layer of energy that attracts objects such as iron and steel toward it.

magnetometer: an instrument that reads the magnetic properties of rock.

magnetosphere: the magnetic force that surrounds Earth.

magnitude: the power of an earthquake, as recorded by a seismograph.

mainshock: the largest tremor of an earthquake.

mantle: a layer of hot rock beneath Earth's crust.

metamorphic rock: rock that has been radically changed by the heat and pressure of mountain building into another type of rock.

meteorologist: a scientist who studies weather and the atmosphere.

microbe: a tiny organism that can only be seen with the aid of a microscope.

mid-ocean ridge: a mountain range beneath the ocean.

mineral: an inorganic (lifeless) substance that contains a definite chemical structure.

molten rock: rock that has been melted by extremely high temperatures within Earth.

mudflow: a destructive flow of melted snow and ice, mixed with loose rock and sediments, which occurs with a volcanic eruption.

mud pot: a spring that flows with clay, mud, and minerals rather than water.

mud volcano: a mud pot around which a cone or mound of hardened mud has formed.

nuée ardente: a high-speed eruption of hot gas, ash, pumice, and bits of rock from a volcano.

oceanography: the study of the oceans.

pahoehoe: smooth lava that cools into a surface that looks like twine.

paint pot: a rare type of mud pot colored bright red or pink from iron in the mud.

Pangaea: the ancient supercontinent, which broke up into the continents that cover Earth today.

permeable rock: rock that contains cracks and openings through which water can enter, such as granite and limestone.

perpetual spouter: a geyser that continuously jets with water and steam, with no quiet periods in between.

pillow lava: pahoehoe lava flowing from volcanoes beneath the sea that forms into sacklike shapes.

planetesimals: rocky objects that collided with each other, stuck together, and grew until they formed an object the size of Earth today.

plate tectonics: a theory to describe the movement of Earth's crust, which explains the cause of earthquakes, volcanoes, and mountain building.

primary waves/P waves: the first shocks felt when an earthquake occurs.

pumice: lava that hardens into lightweight rocks and boulders.

radioactivity: the energy released when atoms break apart.

Rayleigh waves: surface earthquake waves that move the ground up-and-down and side-to-side.

regular geyser: a geyser that erupts on a regular schedule.

reservoir: a small open space within a geyser system that fills up with groundwater.

rhyolite: a type of volcanic rock found in geyser systems.

Richter scale: the method used to measure the strength of an earthquake.

Ring of Fire: the area of high earthquake and volcanic activity on the edges of the Pacific plate.

rock-forming mineral: a substance that binds together to form rock. There are two types of rock-forming minerals: silicates and carbonates.

runoff: rainwater that flows over the surface and does not seep into the ground.

San Andreas Fault: an area along western California where the Pacific plate is moving against the North American plate.

scree: the broken section of a mountain where the rock has been shattered by ice.

seafloor spreading: crust that spreads apart from both sides of a mid-ocean ridge.

seamount: an underwater volcano that does not reach above the surface.

secondary waves/S waves: earthquake body waves that travel more slowly than P waves and that move rock in a side-to-side motion.

sediment: thick layers of rocky material that have settled on the seafloor.

sedimentary rock: rock made of particles of sand and mud or the remainders of plants that have been pressed into layers on lake or sea beds.

seismic wave: energy released from an earthquake.

seismograph: an instrument used to detect and measure seismic waves.

seismology: the science of earthquakes.

shield volcano: a smooth, gently sloped volcano formed by Hawaiian volcanic eruptions.

silicate: the most common mineral found in Earth's crust, made out of oxygen and the element silicon.

sill: magma that seeps into horizontal cracks inside Earth's crust and forms a sheet of igneous rock.

solar system: a group of planets and the star (Sun) around which they revolve.

solar wind: particles of energy streaming from the Sun.

sonar: a system to measure the distance of objects using an echo-sounding device.

strato-volcano: a volcano built up into a cone shape as the result of many violent eruptions.

subduction: the process of one plate of Earth's crust moving beneath another plate.

surface amplification: the increased motion on the surface when earthquake body waves are reflected back into the ground.

surface waves: earthquake shock waves on top of the ground, created by the movement of body waves.

theory: a scientific explanation of why and how something works.

thrust faulting: the breaking apart of layers of oceanic crust as it moves beneath a continental plate; some of the oceanic crust is heaped up onto the continent to form new land and mountain ranges.

tiltmeter: an instrument used to measure changes in the shape of the ground or on the surface of a volcano.

tremor: a shaking movement of Earth that may or may not be felt by people.

vent: an opening in the crust or on a volcano from which magma, water, steam, or gas can erupt.

volcanic: made from a volcano.

volcanic action: the eruption of molten rock from inside Earth up to Earth's surface.

Volcanic Explosivity Index, or **VEI:** a system used to describe the size of volcanic eruptions.

volcano: a mountain formed from the eruption of magma.

volcanologist: a scientist who studies volcanoes.

weathering: the process by which mountains are worn down by natural forces such as wind and rain.

Index

A
aa lava, 76, 77
accretion, 1
aftershock, 54
algae, 9, 10, 108, 110
archaea, 31
ash, 63
atoms, 2
aurora borealis, 7

B
bacteria, 9, 110
basalt, 76
batholith, 79
black smokers, 31
body waves, 48

C
calderas, 74–75, 82, 105
carbonates, 5
centrifugal force, 19
compass, 7
compounds, 2
condensation, 9
cone, 102

continental drift, 16, 27, 29
convection currents, 18, 19
core, 6
crust, 4–5, 15–25. *See also* plate tectonics; vents
crustaceans, 10

D
dike, 79
dinosaurs, 10, 11
duration, 104

E
Earth. *See also* crust; earthquakes; mountains; volcanoes
　formation and structure of, 1–6
　as giant magnet, 6–9, 29–30, 58
　history of, 10–13
earthquakes
　animal behavior before, 57, 58–59, 91
　causes of, 43–48, 62
　as clues to volcanoes, 78
　measuring, 3–4, 49, 51–56